TOPGUN'S
TOP 10

TOPGUN'S TOP 10

LEADERSHIP LESSONS
FROM THE COCKPIT

GUY M. SNODGRASS

Commander, U.S. Navy (Ret.)

CENTER
STREET

New York   Nashville

Center Street
Hachette Book Group
1290 Avenue of the Americas, New York, NY 10104
centerstreet.com
twitter.com/centerstreet

First Edition: September 2020

Center Street is a division of Hachette Book Group, Inc. The Center Street name and logo are trademarks of Hachette Book Group, Inc.

The publisher is not responsible for websites (or their content) that are not owned by the publisher.

The photograph on page xx is by Christopher Michel. Used by permission. All other photographs are either property of the author or provided by the U.S. Navy under the public domain for use without restriction.

Library of Congress Control Number: 2020938832

ISBNs: 978-1-5460-5963-9 (hardcover); 978-1-5460-5962-2 (ebook)

SARAH, your selfless dedication as a military spouse enabled me to live my dreams, even when we had to take a rain check on yours.

TO MY CHILDREN: Ryan, Nathan, and Natalie. Be relentless in discovering and pursuing your passion in life. Always remember, nothing worthwhile is ever easy.

TO THE TOPGUN STAFF: In a world awash in change, your steadfast devotion to maintaining the highest professional standards makes all the difference. Non sibi sed patriae...Not for self, but country.

CONTENTS

"Most of us, most of the time, live in blissful ignorance of what a small elite, heroic group of Americans are doing for us night and day. All over the globe, American Sailors are doing something very dangerous. Somewhere around the world, young men and women are landing Naval aircraft on the pitching decks of aircraft carriers, living on the edge of danger so the rest of us need not think about, let alone experience, danger."

—George Will

Two U.S. Navy F-4 Phantom II fighter aircraft are readied for launch from the flight deck of the attack aircraft carrier USS *John F. Kennedy* (CVA-67) in the 1970s.

INTRODUCTION

66 TOPGUN's precepts have served me
well in and out of uniform, especially
during the most challenging times and
particularly when the path forward
was uncertain. 99

ONE OF TODAY'S most recognizable elite military institutions was born from the crucible of the Vietnam War, when American aviators quickly realized the advantages they'd enjoyed during World War II and the Korean War no longer applied. Worse, during the early days of the Vietnam War, hundreds of American airmen, like U.S. Navy Lt. Cmdr. John S. McCain and Cmdr. James Stockdale, had been shot down by enemy MiG fighter jets, surface-to-air missiles, or ground artillery fire. Because they went on to return home, they were the relatively lucky ones; many others were killed immediately or died in captivity. U.S. Navy pilots, who had grown accustomed to owning the skies during

Introduction

World War II and the Korean War, found themselves at a significant disadvantage this time around.

Something was wrong. Based on their performance during prior conflicts, Navy pilots should have excelled in air-to-air battles. World War II had seen kill ratios of ten to one: ten enemy planes shot down for every American plane. The Korean War demonstrated similar levels of success.

In Vietnam, this number had dropped to less than two to one. Compounding the problem was the Navy's prioritization of newly developed air-to-air missiles and their use with its latest fighter jets, primarily F-4 Phantoms. From June 1965 to September 1968, American pilots fired nearly six hundred missiles at enemy aircraft, with only sixty or so finding their way to the target, a paltry success rate. Aviators worried that an insufficient amount of aircrew training, repeated missile failures, and the Phantom's lack of a machine gun—omitted because the U.S. Navy was convinced dogfighting was a thing of the past—explained why the kill ratio had plummeted.

How many more Americans might suffer the same

Introduction

fate as John McCain and the hundreds of other airmen who had fallen from the sky? To help reverse this tragic turn of events, the Navy turned to Capt. Frank W. Ault, a senior officer in the Pentagon tasked with holistically reviewing what was broken with dogfighting in Vietnam—and, more importantly, devising a plan to fix it. For five months, he and other naval professionals pored over reports to determine how best to restore the U.S. Navy's anemic kill ratio. In January 1969, Captain Ault and his team published the 480-page *Air-to-Air Missile System Capability Review*, later popularly and more succinctly known as the Ault Report.

The report dissected every aspect of the problem and offered concrete solutions for Navy brass to consider. One recommendation stood out: the proposal to create an advanced fighter weapons school at then Naval Air Station Miramar, in San Diego, California, designed to teach aircrew how to not just survive in dogfighting— but to win.

Usually, governments and big institutions move like glaciers, but just two months later, on March 3, 1969, the U.S. Navy Fighter Weapons School opened its doors.

Introduction

You may know the school by a shorter name, correctly written in capitals and all one word: "TOPGUN."

Originally operating out of a ramshackle trailer, instructors begged, borrowed, and stole what they needed to get the school up and running. Short on funds and equipment, they had no other choice but that first cadre made it work. It didn't take long to achieve results.

A TOPGUN-trained aircrew notched its first kill a little over a year later when, on March 28, 1970, Lt. Jerome Beaulier and Lt. (junior grade) Stephen Barkley, flying a U.S. Navy F-4 fighter jet, pumped a missile into a North Vietnamese MiG-21's tailpipe.

Then, in April 1972, North Vietnamese tanks and artillery boldly smashed across the demilitarized zone into South Vietnam. Aiming to disrupt Hanoi's supply lines, the United States responded with Operation Linebacker. In that operation, the U.S. Air Force compiled a meager 1.78-to-1 kill ratio. But aviators from the Navy's Seventh Fleet recorded a thirteen-to-one kill ratio, shooting down twenty-six planes and losing only two.

TOPGUN worked.

But the TOPGUN story didn't end with the pullout

Introduction

of U.S. forces from Vietnam in 1973—that was only the beginning. The school grew in stature with each passing decade. The remainder of the 1970s validated the school's impact, and students and instructors began to train against more capable adversary aircraft, including enemy MiGs brought to America from overseas.

The school went relatively unnoticed by the American public until 1986, when Tom Cruise starred in the original *Top Gun* movie. (He also stars in the 2020 sequel, *Top Gun: Maverick*.) Critics weren't sure what to make of the first movie, but the public loved it from the start—and still does. *Top Gun* proved to be 1986's top-grossing film, packing theaters for a full six months and making it easier for the military to attract new recruits for years.

Tens of millions around the world who saw the movie were now TOPGUN fans.

In 1996, the school moved from Miramar—nicknamed "Fightertown USA"—to Naval Air Station Fallon, located in the Nevada desert seventy miles east of Reno. The changing threat—shifting from overwater engagements against Soviet aircraft during the

Introduction

height of the Cold War to combating Middle Eastern terrorism—made desert training crucial. Although dog-fighting and air-to-air combat remained the school's primary missions, more emphasis was placed on the air-to-ground combat skills aviators would need over Iraq and Afghanistan.

More than fifty years after its founding, TOPGUN still provides select aviators with a graduate-level course designed to produce the world's finest combat aviators. TOPGUN alumni form the cadre of teachers who instruct, influence, and cultivate talent across the U.S. Navy and Marine Corps (as both services are included within the Department of the Navy).

To succeed in this unrelenting training course, students—typically junior officers in their mid-twenties and fresh off their very first tour of duty—must possess three key attributes: talent, passion, and personality. Mastering each is crucial. Throughout the twelve-week course, the knowledge, skills, and aerial tactics needed to fight and win our nation's wars are drilled into the men and women who will one day comprise the top one percent of military fighter pilots. Those asked to remain

Introduction

as TOPGUN instructors, typically only two or three students from a class of fifteen or more, must uphold an even higher—and more unrelenting—standard.

Despite its emphasis on peerless flight training in fighter jets, TOPGUN develops one critical trait above all others: leadership. And it starts from day one.

IN 2006, I had the honor of becoming a TOPGUN graduate and then spending three years as an instructor—an awe-inspiring and humbling experience.

Monday through Saturday, incredibly talented sailors and marines arrived at the U.S. Fighter Weapons School ready to push their personal boundaries to achieve their fullest potential. While we recognized that perfection is impossible to attain, we also subscribed to the idea that getting better every day was the goal.

Be better today than yesterday.

Do the same tomorrow.

My path to TOPGUN was similar to the paths followed by the hundreds of others who'd already attended. Like many, I fell in love with aviation at a young age.

Aircraft taxiing toward the bow catapults on USS *Enterprise*'s flight deck in preparation for the day's flight operations.

Introduction

One of the elders for the church I attended worked for General Dynamics, a military contractor producing F-16 fighter jets for the U.S. military. Knowing that I was interested in aviation, he routinely brought me posters with "glamour shots" of the plane, which I hung on the walls of my room. My Boy Scout troop also held an annual fundraiser during airshows at Alliance Airport, an airfield located just to the northwest of the Dallas–Fort Worth metroplex. I watched with utter fascination as the U.S. Air Force Thunderbirds and U.S. Navy Blue Angels amazed crowds with their precise maneuvers and out-of-this-world skill level. The energy, excitement, and jet noise were all I needed—I was hooked.

But getting to flight training was the first of many challenging steps. In high school my grades were only slightly above average, and I was a mediocre varsity cross-country runner. Not exactly the standout that my first choice for college—the U.S. Naval Academy—was looking for. Fortunately for me, the congressional selection committee (most students require a nomination from a congressman or senator to attend) were swayed by my demonstrated leadership achievements.

Introduction

I had earned my Eagle Scout, had led my Scouting troop, and was the only volunteer student member serving on Colleyville's City Council. I'd even started our city's first-ever recycling program, something ahead of its time in Northern Texas in the early 1990s.

Things fell into place. In 1994, I was accepted to college at the U.S. Naval Academy and graduated high school. Four years later I became a naval officer chosen to attend pilot training upon graduating from the Academy. I was also selected as one of fifteen officers afforded the chance to earn a master's degree before training. So I applied to and was selected to attend the Massachusetts Institute of Technology, where I earned two master's degrees: one in nuclear engineering and the other in computer science (a testament to the incredible opportunities provided by a military career).

After graduating from MIT in 2000, I headed off to Pensacola, Florida, to begin my training as a naval aviator. For the next two years, I rapidly worked my way through various initial training stops—flight training with the U.S. Air Force in Oklahoma and more advanced jet training with the U.S. Navy in Mississippi and California—on my path toward becoming a fleet F/A-18 fighter pilot. I graduated first in my class and prepared to join "the fleet" with the U.S. Navy.

In 2003, my first operational tour of duty took me to Virginia and included seven months onboard an aircraft carrier bound for Operation Iraqi Freedom in the Persian Gulf. I flew dozens of combat missions over Iraq: conducting surveillance, guarding friendly troops on the ground, and attacking enemy positions as U.S. forces sought to retake the Iraqi city of Fallujah. When my squadron's time in the Middle East was over, the aircraft carrier returned us to Virginia, where we resumed our normal day-to-day training.

My idol growing up had been Chuck Yeager, the U.S. Air Force test pilot who, in 1947, became the first person to fly faster than the speed of sound. I'd thought about following in his footsteps but soon learned that modern-day test pilots no longer pushed the envelope as radically as they did in the 1960s, 1970s, and 1980s. In the face of this reality and seeking to explore the limits of my own tactical abilities, I applied to become a TOPGUN instructor. Handpicked to attend by the current TOPGUN staff, I

Introduction

left my squadron months earlier than scheduled to begin my new adventure, a path that incurred an additional five-year commitment.

Leaving my first squadron eight months early meant I had logged fewer flight hours in the cockpit than my peers, but I was ready and willing to put in the time and effort required to reach my fullest potential. I soon learned that my instructors were more than happy to provide the training and mentorship I needed while upholding their famously unrelenting standards. Ultimately, my time at TOPGUN made me a far better naval officer, fighter pilot, and leader.

In the years that followed, I returned to the fleet as commander of my own fighter squadron, where I focused on applying the key lessons from my time at TOPGUN and systematically compiled them in a way to convey them to others. I shared these with the sailors in my Japan-based fighter squadron, and they took these lessons to heart. Together, we earned the 2017 Battle Efficiency Award as the top-ranked Navy fighter squadron. I continued to share these lessons during my tenure working for Secretary of Defense James Mattis in the

Introduction

Pentagon and with companies and organizations since my retirement from active duty. TOPGUN's precepts have served me well in and out of uniform, especially during the most challenging times and particularly when the path forward was uncertain.

TOPGUN'S TOP 10: Leadership Lessons from the Cockpit is distilled from the lessons that some of America's greatest patriots taught me. Their wisdom made all the difference in my own journey. I hope it makes a positive difference in yours.

The author (back row, second from left) with the other members of his TOPGUN class in front of a F-16N aggressor before graduation in 2006.

READ BEFORE FLIGHT

> 66 Pro tip: avoid passing out while flying a
> jet at the speed of sound. 99

BRIGHT, ALMOST BLINDING, sunlight seeps over the horizon, highlighting members of a maintenance crew moving between fighter jets on the crowded flight line.

It's early morning in western Nevada's remote Stillwater Mountains. Most of the maintainers—Navy-speak for maintenance personnel—had arrived before dawn to perform crucial safety inspections on jet engines, hydraulic systems, and radars as well as to load 100-pound training missiles for the day's hectic flight schedule.

Farther down the flight line, a low, moaning whine starts. A jet engine fires up for preflight checks, the sound slowly building to a deafening crescendo before rapidly settling into an idling's steady wail. Minutes later, the sound cuts off as the engine shuts down, maintenance preflight checks completed.

I'm in an adjacent building finishing a flight briefing with other aircrew—the U.S. Navy term covering both fighter pilots and weapons systems officers. (All fighter jets require a pilot, but some jets have two seats, one directly behind the other. In this situation, the pilot flies the plane from the front seat while the weapons systems officer helps with task loading by running the radar, radio, and other electronics from the back seat.) We had arrived before dawn to prepare for the day's first wave of flights. I headed into my assigned briefing room to write the live-or-die flight details on a large whiteboard to guide my instructor through this morning's dogfight against two "enemy" aircraft. After his questions had been answered, we departed the room to down a final cup of coffee before heading to the hangar.

Propelling a high-performance jet into flight isn't easy. The hangar team insists you read through the aircraft's maintenance logs and sign for the aircraft. It's like renting a car—only this vehicle costs $78 million and can go from zero to 200 miles per hour in two seconds when launched from an aircraft carrier. Signing for the jet requires an eye attuned to detail for sifting through page after page of information, including the types of missiles loaded and any problems that may have been encountered during the plane's previous ten flights. Either everything checks out or you don't sign.

Flying a fighter jet requires highly specialized flight gear: a flight helmet with tinted visor, a pressurized G-suit (special pants worn over my flight suit), and the survival gear all military aviators must wear while flying. Today's dogfight necessitates that I tightly cinch the G-suit to counter the increased gravity created at high speeds. We call them "speed jeans" for use when we "pull Gs." Zigzagging a jet aggressively during dogfights causes blood to rush from the head and pool in the legs. The G-suit inflates automatically when it senses high-G flight, forcing blood back toward your head to help prevent you from passing out.

Read Before Flight

' Pro tip: avoid passing out while flying a jet at the speed of sound.

With my flight gear strapped on, I grab my helmet and head out to the flight line where row after row of jets await. All that's left is to start the engines, run through my preflight checklists, taxi to the runway, and take off.

Today's flight will last about two hours: forty-five minutes on the flight line to start the engines and preflight checks, followed by an hour of airborne dogfighting over the Nevada desert. Once back on solid ground, I perform each of the previous steps in reverse: taking off my flight gear, signing the jet back to the maintenance team, and heading back to the classroom to debrief.

This entire sequence—preparation, brief, flight, and debrief—requires more than seven hours to complete, a process instructors usually undergo multiple times a day, often six days a week. (Students only have one event per day to allow for intense study and preparation time.)

Aviators at TOPGUN invest thousands of hours studying, preparing, and honing their flight skills. They use flight simulators to fight artificial battles; at other times, they launch themselves skyward in real jets— all in a never-ending pursuit for excellence. *They don't stop until they get it right. That's how they become the finest in the world.*

The best.

A U.S. Navy F/A-18E Super Hornet just prior to landing on the nuclear-powered aircraft carrier USS *George Washington* (CVN-73) during a 2014 Pacific patrol.

CHAPTER ONE

FOCUS ON TALENT, PASSION, AND PERSONALITY

> 66 There's a common refrain about dogfighting: lose sight and you lose the fight. 99

IT'S JULY 25, 2005. A ground crew member responsible for my jet ran onto the flight line holding yellow chocks—two twelve-inch pieces of wood painted yellow and connected with a short rope—that he slid both in front of and behind my F/A-18C Hornet's tires to prevent the jet from rolling forward. I watched him from the cockpit and, with good reason, slumped down into my ejection seat. I wanted it to swallow me up.

I had just failed my "rush ride" at TOPGUN. The rush ride was my audition, a dogfight with a current instructor and my test to see if I'd qualify as a TOPGUN instructor.

What a waste of time, I thought. I'd prepared for

3

months, reading everything I could about dogfighting. I'd pored through the TOPGUN Manual—the bible for Navy and Marine Corps fighter pilots. I'd spent hour after hour watching and rewatching videos on the art of dogfighting recorded by a TOPGUN instructor. I'd even traveled from my home base in Virginia Beach, Virginia, to Fallon, Nevada, just for today's flight.

The morning had started well. I'd spent a month rehearsing my briefing, and it had flowed smoothly. Before the actual flight, my instructor seemed pleased and even offered me a few compliments. Using small model aircraft attached to the end of long wooden rods, he provided me with some pointers on how to more effectively teach some of the most difficult aspects of our flight. Using these models enables the briefer to show aircrew how the jets should maneuver rather than just telling them the positional relationship expected during flight. Briefing complete, we had headed out to the flight line. I was pumped.

We had three simulated dogfights scheduled for that day. But by the end of our second dogfight, I was thoroughly deflated.

Focus on Talent, Passion, and Personality

The first set of maneuvers went poorly, with the instructor—flying the "red enemy" jet against me—rapidly positioning his fighter jet to where he could launch simulated missiles and knock me from the sky. I attributed my swift defeat to bad luck: I'd kept sight of his aircraft the entire time (always a good thing) but felt sluggish in my own jet, seemingly unable to counter the aggressive maneuvers he employed to gain the advantage.

The second set ended just like the first.

Like two cars traveling together on a highway, our aircraft started within sight of each other, only a mile apart and headed in the same direction. We needed to maneuver our aircraft away from each other to start the fight, so I flipped a small switch on the jet's throttle to key the mic and made a radio call using our flight's call sign for the day: "Showtime, take a cut away."

With those words, our three-dimensional dance began. We pointed our jets 30 degrees away from each other. We drifted apart for the next ten seconds: a mile and a half, two miles, two and a half miles. His aircraft grew smaller in the distance. We were three miles apart when I made my next radio call using my specific call sign for this flight: "Showtime one-one, turning in," a call to let my instructor know that I was turning my jet back toward him.

The earphones in my helmet crackled to life as the instructor responded using his assigned call sign for the day: "Showtime one-two, turning in…visual."

We pointed our jets straight at each other in a head-to-head engagement called high-aspect basic fighter maneuvers, the most dynamic type of dogfight. With each of us traveling at 530 miles per hour, the distance between us was now closing rapidly. Ten seconds later, we met at the "merge"—the term for the location and moment in time when our aircraft sped past each other in opposite directions like cars passing on a two-lane road.

I threw the control stick hard to the left, rolling the aircraft to its side; paused briefly before pulling the stick back toward my lap; and began a high-G maneuver to cut a hard, level turn across the horizon. My body ached from pulling seven Gs. My arm, which normally weighs ten pounds, now experienced seventy pounds of force, all pulling it toward my lap. With this amount of force working against my entire body, I found it nearly impossible to turn my head to look around.

I strained to watch as my instructor flew upward, placing his jet between me and the sun. Suddenly, he vanished—a sound strategy, designed to force his adversary (me) to stare directly into the sun, making it nearly impossible to see.

Oh, no…where'd he go? I growled under my breath as I keyed the mic, before saying "Blind…sun," a mandatory safety call to let him know I could no longer see him. "Roger, continue" was his only reply. Was he gloating? His radio call confirmed he could still see me. He would exploit my weakness to close in for the kill.

My eyes filled with tears from staring into the sun. All I could do was blink to clear them away. Seconds later—a *lifetime* during aerial combat—I found him again. He had deftly maneuvered his jet back downhill, aiming to arrive behind me as we waged three-dimensional combat. I was now on the defensive—and I knew it.

I toggled another switch on the throttle to dispense

flares from underneath my jet while pulling toward him, hoping to make it more difficult for him to fire a missile at me. An AIM-9 Sidewinder heat-seeking missile would be his weapon of choice due to our close proximity, as he had closed to within a mile behind my jet. But would he do that? Or would he use the six-barrel Gatling gun mounted in his jet's nose?

I twisted my back and neck in an attempt to keep him in view. There's a common refrain about dogfighting: lose sight and you lose the fight. If you can't spot your adversary, then you can't fight them, and before you know it, you're taking a missile up your tailpipe.

I had to think fast. My instructor was still behind my aircraft and likely to take a shot at any second. I needed to force my instructor into a more neutral maneuver called the "flat scissors," a position where he would be flying more to the left or right side of my aircraft rather than planted firmly behind me. This would require him to misjudge his speed and fly past me, my only real opportunity to turn the tables.

He didn't budge.

A few seconds later, I heard his voice in my helmet:

Focus on Talent, Passion, and Personality

"Fox-2...kill Hornet in a right-hand turn," a radio call announcing that he'd fired a simulated heat-seeking Sidewinder missile into my jet. Game over for the second dogfight.

Our third set went better, as I was able to hold him off longer than during the first two engagements, but ended similarly. My instructor won for the third time in a row. I shook my head. Could it get any worse?

Running low on fuel, we stopped dogfighting and rejoined into formation, turning southwest toward Naval Air Station Fallon, Nevada, TOPGUN's home base.

We took turns performing battle damage checks, flying with our wingtips only a few feet away from each other—at times as close together as the Blue Angel or Thunderbird flight demonstration teams are during their air show performances. We inspected each other's aircraft to ensure all panels and components were still attached—something not to be taken for granted after maneuvering dynamically and under heavy Gs. During my first tour of duty I'd seen everything from small, inert practice bombs to aircraft panels ripped off aircraft while flying. A lot can happen when your plane's speed is close to—or often beyond—the speed of sound.

As the lead pilot, I was responsible for bringing us back in for landing, so I maneuvered my jet to point us in the right direction. Soon enough, we could see the airfield. The scenery was breathtaking as our jets swooped down over the salty white sands of the valley below, the Stillwater Mountain range just off to our east. We switched our radios to the airfield control tower's frequency.

"Fallon Tower, Showtime one-one…flight of two F-18s, field in sight." There was momentary silence as control tower personnel scanned the skies with their binoculars searching for us. Soon, they responded with "Showtime one-one, Fallon Tower, we have you in sight. You are cleared to land runway Three-One Left."

I received clearance and quickly stowed my loose gear into a bag stuffed beside me in the cockpit. I didn't want to apply the brakes after touching down on the runway only to have a pen or some other small item shoot forward and land on the floor. With so little space available in a fighter jet's cockpit, you could spend days trying to find and recover it...and no one is allowed to fly the aircraft until you do, lest the offending item break free during a future flight and jam the throttles or control stick.

Wheels greasing the runway, we landed about twenty seconds apart. We then taxied off the runway and back to our assigned jet parking spots where our plane captains awaited us, chocks in hand.

Based on my poor performance, I dreaded meeting with my instructor.

I had flopped.

He didn't say much as we checked our aircraft in with maintenance and removed our flight gear. The silence was murder. Finally, I announced I was heading back to the briefing room to prepare for the debrief. He simply nodded, acknowledging me by my personal call sign, "Sure, Bus, see you in a few."

About thirty minutes later he joined me to talk about the flight. As the lead pilot (and student), I was responsible for conducting the debrief.

Sure, I had performed poorly, but I still had a job to do. I fell back on years of training, stoically and methodically walking the instructor through all aspects of the flight. I brought up a few items I had omitted from the preflight brief that would have improved our outcome. I reconstructed each of our performances from memory—all three engagements. We then watched videos recorded from inside the aircraft to compare factual data against my memory, always important because perceptions can change over time and while flying at high speeds. Invariably, aircrew will miss something. ***Comparing perception with reality is crucial.***

As I finished, I wrote on the whiteboard all of the major items we needed to improve for future flights. We are trained to hold nothing back, so I wrote down a long laundry list for both of us. Needless to say, my list was quite a bit longer than his list.

It was now my instructor's turn to share with me what I had missed. And, more importantly, he needed to share how we could both improve our next flight. I steadied myself, preparing for the worst after such a poor showing in the jet.

Standing before the whiteboard, he considered

my notes before turning around. "Overall," he said, "I thought you did very well. Nice job."

Huh? I lost all three sets. You shot me down every time. Why are you saying I did a nice job?

He paused a few moments before continuing. "You have a lot to learn, but no one shows up to a rush ride and defeats their instructor. I've had years of additional training and spent hundreds of hours focusing on becoming the very best I can be at dogfighting. You briefed well. You have solid flight leadership skills and flew well overall. The rest can be learned with time. So, well done. I think you should come here and be a TOP-GUN instructor."

I could hardly believe it. "I'm honored," I stammered, "but why? Surely there are far better candidates based on my performance during our flight."

What he said next has remained with me ever since: "Because it's not purely about ability, Bus. At TOPGUN we evaluate instructors based on three criteria—*talent, passion,* and *personality.* Yes, talent is required. You have it...and we'll make you much better. But passion and personality are just as important. Your preparation was well above average and shows that you really care about doing your best. Despite the way the fight turned out, you came back to the debrief and called it like it was. You didn't try to spin me or make up excuses. You could be the most talented fighter pilot in the world, but if you aren't passionate about tactics and if people dislike you, well, you'd never be respected as an instructor. ***Remember: none of us wins a hundred percent of the time. Your credibility is far more important.*"**

We shook hands as he left the room. I'd have to wait another month for official notification, but I was elated when the news came. I was going to be a TOPGUN instructor.

So often in life we focus on *what we want* rather than *who we are*. My instructor was spot-on. In every one of my tours of duty following TOPGUN—from aircraft carriers to the Pentagon—no one cared whether I won or lost on any particular issue. They cared far more about being around someone who simply wanted to make each day better than the one before and who could help them achieve their fullest potential—someone whom they respected.

Focus on Talent, Passion, and Personality

Each day brings a million different distractions, each one competing to knock you off your game. This is especially true in today's "always-on" social media environment. It can be easy to lose sight of who you are, what you stand for, and what you care about. You have to finds ways to cut down on the noise and focus on what really matters.

Whether you're still a student, starting a new job, a senior leader in a company, or somewhere in between, never lose sight of the basics. Make time to invest in yourself. When adversity strikes—as it always does—refocus your determination and try again. Commit to making each day better than the one before. Then do it again the next day. In the long run, people care far more about *who* you are than *what* you do.

Make your talent, passion, and personality your calling card.

Two U.S. Navy F/A-18E Super Hornets from Strike Fighter Squadron ONE NINE FIVE fly past the nuclear-powered aircraft carrier USS *George Washington* in 2015. The author is piloting the aircraft closest to the camera.

CHAPTER TWO

NOTHING WORTHWHILE IS EVER EASY

> 66 …the standard is *the standard*. It is
> unflinching and unforgiving. 99

ONE OF THE first responsibilities assigned to a new TOPGUN instructor is to become *the* subject-matter expert for a particular specialty. Topics include dogfighting, aerial combat, attacking ground targets, the specifics of enemy aircraft, other nations' missile-defense systems, aerial radars, advanced training, and many more—in all, approximately thirty subjects that turn into TOPGUN classroom lectures. Each instructor is expected to master one of these highly technical areas. Heady stuff for a staff consisting mostly of junior officers fresh off their first tours of fleet duty—a requirement for admission with few exceptions.

Incredibly, these staff members, twenty-five in all,

set the aerial combat standards for the entire U.S. Navy and Marine Corps—approximately 339,000 sailors and 185,000 marines. A single person is the recognized expert for more than a half-million service members. The pressure to perform is high…and starts from day one.

Decades ago, TOPGUN graduates returned immediately to the fleet to continue their tours before being selected to return as instructors. In each class, only a few aviators were themselves destined to become TOPGUN instructors. Now, students are identified as possible staff members before they arrive; they receive additional scrutiny while training and become instructors the day they graduate.

Shortly after I finished the course, senior TOPGUN instructors pulled me into an office to inform me which area I'd be expected to learn about and then teach. Four lectures were due for rotation, and each needed a new instructor. Which would I be assigned?

Rotations and assignments are carefully timed, a consideration made more important as TOPGUN teaches only three classes per year. Proper timing provides continuity for the staff, as senior instructors pass along experience and knowledge to junior ones. The staff needed the new team members to commence our training in order to replace instructors due to leave within six to eight months.

I was thrilled to be assigned air-to-air mission planning, considered by instructors to be one of the staff's more important and difficult lectures. My assignment was due to timing more than anything else but also in part because I'd attended graduate school for engineering at MIT, since math and risk management make up the foundation for air-to-air mission planning. The weight of the assignment hit me when I learned the nickname for the process I was expected to master: *the murderboard*.

A murderboard is the recitation of the entire lecture that will ultimately be presented to the students, but first it is presented to the rest of the instructors to ensure new candidates are ready—TOPGUN's equivalent of defending a PhD dissertation. In my case, I'd be required to stand in front of fifty current and former instructors and present a 236-slide, four-hour lecture— all from memory.

That's one aspect that makes TOPGUN's murder-board process unique: the briefer isn't allowed to refer to notes or even *look* at the slides (although rare exceptions are made if, for example, referring to a chart). My murderboard was already tentatively scheduled for six months down the road. It was time to get to work.

I couldn't help but consider the situation. *How in the world will I ever be able to give a four-hour presentation from memory?*

The task seemed daunting. Compounding the pressure was the expectation from senior instructors that I would simultaneously maintain a robust flight schedule. Large chunks of each day would be consumed flying missions as "red air" (simulating enemy aircraft) against the new crop of students.

To help new instructors conquer this assignment, the staff created the "pre-board process." Each new instructor has four months to research their topic, work with the outgoing instructor expert, develop new recommendations, and create their own presentation. In my case, the previous expert had already departed, so I learned primarily by studying the slides he had left behind. He did visit periodically, and we found time for me to question him on the fundamentals of aerial combat—in my case, creating procedures to be used by aircrew when fighting against other aircraft.

The daily schedule initially proved hectic. Typically, I'd arrive before dawn to fly the day's first red air mission. Once I had flown and debriefed the first mission, I'd grab a quick bite for lunch before hustling in for the red air briefing for a second flight. After the second flight and debrief, I was off to my desk to study for several more hours. Soon, this routine—one or two flights per day followed by murderboard preparation—became second nature.

My first four months on the staff flew by. Before I knew it, I was asked to give my first pre-board, the first of eight practice lectures taught to a small number of instructors.

The bar for each pre-board is high, but it's intended to help new instructors improve through incredibly specific feedback on every aspect of the lecture. Of course, it didn't always feel this way when I was on the receiving end. For my first pre-board, three senior TOPGUN instructors sat around a conference table to observe and evaluate. I had to provide each with a stack of "critique sheets," formatted so an instructor could quickly spot an error, write down the corresponding slide number, and describe the error and its needed correction.

Feedback covered *everything*. Was there a typo on the slide? Caught and recorded. When I forgot part of my presentation and needed to sneak a glance at the slide to remember where I was, they annotated "slide peek" to remind me where I had stumbled. They noted when I tried to teach a concept that didn't make sense or was unclear. Fillers like "uh" or "um" were forbidden. Nothing escaped their attention.

My first pre-board didn't go well. I stumbled through many of the concepts and needed to turn and look at the slides more than a dozen times. Some of the built-in questions I used to test attendees' knowledge were so poorly worded that the instructors didn't understand what I was asking or how to respond. By the time we finished the four-hour ordeal, each instructor had amassed more than ten pages of notes. One instructor caught more than 150 errors I'd made during the presentation.

Nothing Worthwhile Is Ever Easy

I felt wiped out, mentally and physically, and that was before we even started *their* debrief of my lecture.

When my debrief ended (ninety challenging minutes later), two instructors departed to resume their day's schedule. The third instructor, the same one who had flown my rush ride to get into TOPGUN, hung back to chat with me as I stood by the conference room door.

Patting me on the shoulder, he said, "Bus, never forget…nothing worthwhile is ever easy. Pre-boards are an extremely tough process by design." It was obvious he knew I was unhappy with my performance. "We purposely break you down," he continued, "so we can build you back up. Every one of us here has worked their way through it. Trust me, there's nothing special about any of us. If we can do it, so can you." With a final slap on the back, he headed out to leave me alone with my thoughts.

I sat down at the conference table. Collecting all the notes on the table, I slowly thumbed through each page. "Missile misspelled on slide 16," one comment read.

"Slow start," wrote another instructor. "You sounded robotic until slide 14."

"You looked behind yourself twice on slide 138—spend more time practicing this part," wrote a third.

A light bulb went on for me. There was no doubt that being in the spotlight was painful. The pre-board process ensured I couldn't hide any of my flaws. Everything was fair game, from the slides I'd created to my mannerisms to the tidiness of my uniform. Even the way I held a wooden pointer while teaching about aircraft maneuvers was open to criticism.

But as I took a closer look at their feedback, I realized every comment was blunt and straightforward—none was cruel or mean. It wasn't personal. These instructors were helping me identify every area that needed to be tweaked, corrected, practiced, or reworked to help me be the *best* instructor I could possibly be. Every slide typo caught by an instructor now would be corrected long before I gave my murderboard. The TOPGUN staff's process was obvious: iron sharpens iron. They were doing me a favor by holding me to an incredibly high standard, whether it was my very first pre-board or the very last. The meaning was clear: the standard is *the standard*. It is unflinching and unforgiving.

Nothing Worthwhile Is Ever Easy

Cracking this code restored my motivation. Day after day, I slowly improved. I made note cards representing every slide in my lecture. Based on a helpful hint from another instructor, I separated the cards into manageable chunks representing the five parts of my presentation. I practiced in the car while driving to work in the morning, then again while returning home at night. The sheer magnitude of the overall lecture seemed daunting, but I found that it appeared more manageable when I broke it into bite-sized pieces. That realization helped build my confidence.

Soon, it was time for my murderboard, a day I'll always remember. Traditionally, instructors bring in breakfast snacks and beverages to feed staff members before the lecture. The food I brought felt like a sacrificial offering to the angry murderboard gods; their decision about whether I had passed the test would determine my fate.

My stomach churned as I watched the other instructors file in. I'm fair-skinned and could feel the heat creep into my temples as I flushed with nervousness. But I persevered, moving toward the door for the mandatory countdown. Glancing at my watch, I barked, "Thirty seconds!" while closing the door. Slowly returning to the podium, I stole a second glance to verify my timing. "Ten seconds...five, four, three, two, one...and hack." "Hack" being the term for marking the exact GPS time and a technique used to guarantee everyone in the room was precisely in sync.

To ensure we are able to maintain eye contact with the audience, we're required to avoid looking at the keyboard. So, without looking down, I reached over with my left hand and pressed the Enter key to bring up my first slide. I began my memorized introduction by saying, "The Chinese Air Force experienced an incredibly low kill ratio at the beginning of World War II. Enter U.S. Army Capt. Claire Chenault, who in 1941 formed the First American Volunteer Group, more commonly known by their nickname, the Flying Tigers...."

I shared a story to explain the vital importance of air-to-air mission planning before launching into my first slides about key concepts and definitions. Within a few minutes, I felt the heat recede from my face as months of training and practice kicked into gear. I was off and running.

A few hours later, I received the verdict: I had passed with flying colors.

TOPGUN's arduous process paid off. I had successfully presented a four-hour lecture from memory—a seemingly unthinkable task just six months ago. I had scaled my personal Everest.

The murderboard experience taught me the power of perseverance. It trained me to dig deep, to tap into reserves of strength I never knew I had.

TOPGUN instructors aren't superhuman. Once upon a time, we were all typical, confused high school students. Few of us had graduated as class valedictorian. Many of us had even found ourselves in trouble at various times during our youth. But here we all were, aviators united by a common desire to be the best we could be. ***With direction, teamwork, and a universal adherence to unflinching standards, we made it.***

It's easy to get bogged down and feel overwhelmed when faced with adversity or a seemingly insurmountable task. Who hasn't rested their head in their hands while studying for a big exam or thrown their arms into the air with frustration after a particularly tough episode at work? Upon reflection, though, we realize these are simply fleeting moments in time. Continue to rely on your hard work, dedication, and pursuit of excellence to carry you through. Recognize that there are no shortcuts. Tackle your tough problems head-on and continue to strive for success that sometimes seems just a little out of reach. You have to earn your success…each and every day.

Make today better than yesterday.

Do the same tomorrow.

Just remember, ***nothing worthwhile is ever easy.***

A steam catapult launches an F/A-18 off the flight deck of USS *Carl Vinson*, a nuclear-powered aircraft carrier.

The author preparing his fighter jet prior to takeoff for a training flight in 2009.

CHAPTER THREE

STAY CALM UNDER PRESSURE

> 66 Remember, no matter what is occurring around you: slow is steady, steady is smooth, and smooth is fast—you will accomplish more by remaining calm under pressure. 99

I WAS IN A tight left turn, flying at sixteen thousand feet at full afterburner in Restricted Area 2508, a training range in the airspace over Death Valley National Park in southeastern California, when my airplane suddenly shuddered.

What the hell was that?

A second later, the headphones in my helmet crackled to life. "Engine fire, right...engine fire, right."

Flying behind my aircraft, the flight instructor I'd just been dogfighting saw something I couldn't: a fifteen-foot stream of fire pouring from the exhaust of my right engine.

I was seconds away from possible death, and I

needed to stop the fight. I carefully leveled the wings of my F/A-18C Hornet fighter, my right hand nudging the control stick as my left hand pulled both jet engine throttles back into a midrange position. What next?

Aviate. Navigate. Communicate.

First, aviate. Ensure the aircraft's safety along with the lives of everyone on board. As a single-seat fighter pilot, I had only one life to worry about—my own. Luckily, I was over a remote part of California, so there was little risk of crashing into a populated area.

Second, navigate. A basic principle of flying is to maintain the ability to arrive safely at your destination, even under the most extreme circumstances.

Third, communicate. Never use the radio until you've accomplished the first two steps, as it's by far the least critical of the three rules. Many pilots have lost their lives because they focused on unimportant tasks—like talking on the radio—instead of concentrating on the most important function: safe operation of the aircraft toward the desired destination.

Priorities matter.

I scanned the instruments by my left knee: my right

engine had flatlined at zero rpm, so it was no longer operational, and the right fire warning light was glowing bright red. There are twenty emergencies a pilot can encounter that are so dangerous that aviators are required to memorize a list of steps called "immediate action items" to help them survive. In the preflight brief, failure to recite the list verbatim meant the pilot was grounded. The inability to execute each step in the correct order could be the difference between life and death. An engine fire is one of those potentially deadly emergencies.

Something in me clicked.

Step one: set both throttles to the minimum power setting practical while continuing to assess the situation. Check. Step two: slowly pull the right engine lever all the way back to turn it off. Check. Step three: lift the protective cover and press the FIRE button, cutting off fuel that could cause an explosion. Check. Step four: press the button to activate the fire extinguisher inside the right engine compartment before moving on to step five: putting down the handle for my arresting hook. Check...and check. Glancing back at my instruments, I noticed the right engine fire light was out—a good sign, indicating the fire extinguisher had likely done its job correctly.

I needed to make an emergency landing at the nearest airfield, using the plane's tailhook to catch a wire strung across the runway for just such situations. This would bring the plane to a quick halt so firefighters could spray fire-suppressant foam on the jet after I had shut off the left engine.

Arrested landings are part of every Navy fighter pilot's training—they come with the territory. The runway on an aircraft carrier (called the landing area) is only slightly longer than a football field, so a tailhook is used to stop the aircraft before it runs out of runway and into the water. One second before landing you're flying along; then, wham! You're thrown violently forward in your seat as the wheels touch down, the hook catching and slowing you from 150 mph to a standstill in less than two seconds.

I was now out of immediate danger, but the aircraft was slowly and steadily losing altitude. The military airfield at my home base in Lemoore, California, was too far away to reach safely, so I banked the plane to the right and pointed it toward Naval Air Weapons Station China Lake, in California's western Mojave Desert region. Located about 150 miles north of Los Angeles, it was much closer.

My wingman flew his plane over to my right side to take a closer look. "Raider 21, it looks like the fire is out." *Well, at least I'm not about to explode.*

I reached over, next to my right hip, to where my green helmet bag was located. About two inches thick and made of a fireproof cloth, it has the rough dimensions of a pizza box. I unzipped the top and rummaged through the contents. Finally feeling what I was searching for, I pulled out my pocket checklist to prepare for the emergency landing.

A few minutes later, after verifying that I had completed all required steps, I keyed the mic. "China Lake Tower, this is Raider 21, emergency aircraft."

There was a brief hiss of static before the control tower answered. "Raider 21, China Lake Tower, we copy your emergency. Go ahead." I took a deep breath. No matter what was happening inside the cockpit, I had to sound calm, cool, and collected on the radio. A calm demeanor was contagious and led to better decision making.

"China Lake Tower, Raider 21. I had a right-engine fire and need an immediate arrested landing. One soul on board. Thirty minutes of fuel remaining. Fire is out."

The tower answered right back. "Copy all, Raider 21. No traffic between you and the airport. Fire trucks are rolling."

Twelve minutes later, I spotted the airfield, just to the right of the airplane's nose. I had never been happier to find a place to land. "Tower, Raider 21. Field in sight."

"Raider 21, you are cleared for landing runway three. Arresting gear is in battery." That let me know the wire was now raised on the runway so my tailhook would be able to catch it. With my landing gear already down, I gently banked the F/A-18 to the right and started my descent.

Flying a two-engine jet with a single engine is challenging. The plane has half its normal power, making it harder to gain altitude if needed. Since the right engine was shut down, the thrust from the left engine kept pushing the plane's nose to the right. It felt like trying to drive a car along an icy road—I never quite knew precisely where I was going to wind up, requiring constant flight control inputs to maintain a straight flight path.

I touched down about five minutes later, small puffs of smoke appearing as the wheels hit the runway, the hook catching the wire and bringing me to an abrupt stop. I quickly shut down the left engine. Only then did I notice my legs were trembling—the most obvious sign of the adrenaline that was coursing through my body. I unstrapped my harness and made my way out of the cockpit as firefighters ensured the fire was out.

Walking around the plane to the right side, I could see the damage: oil splashed up the right side of the aircraft, all the way to the nose. What the heck had happened here? How could oil be this far forward on the jet when I was moving at hundreds of miles an hour? The firefighters assured me there was no danger, so I climbed into the engine's intake on the right side of the plane to take a look. Using my fingers, I slowly rotated the fan blades of the engine. It sounded like someone had poured a can of marbles into the engine. After a quarter turn the blades seized. They would never move again.

The engine was trashed.

Two weeks later, I received the findings of the official investigation: someone had left a small rag in the engine as it was being rebuilt. By sheer dumb luck, I'd been the first pilot to fly the plane after the rebuilt engine was installed. The rag had popped loose inside the oil system, causing a catastrophic overpressure in the engine, which is why oil had sprayed all over the right side of the jet. It got so hot that titanium bolts inside the engine warped and melted. (The melting point of titanium is more than 3000°F.) A $70 million aircraft had nearly been lost because one person hadn't done his or her job correctly. Since that person worked in another organization, I never met them or learned of their fate.

More importantly, by remaining calm under pressure, I had ensured that the aircraft and my life were saved during an emergency situation.

I didn't realize it at the time, but the experience would forever pay dividends as I progressed throughout my career. ***Whether handling high-stress situations***

Stay Calm Under Pressure

in combat over the skies of Iraq, intercepting Russian bombers off the coast of South Korea, or "flying a desk" in the Pentagon, staying calm while under fire always proved to be a valuable skill.

The reality is "calm breeds calm." As you progress in life and in your career, you will likely gain increased authority and greater leadership opportunities. Those you lead, whether you realize it or not, are always looking to you to set the example. What signals are you sending? If you remain calm under pressure, they will too. If you panic, they are much more likely to lose confidence. Remaining calm works even during the most stressful and fast-paced of times, a situation made all more real by the 2019–2020 coronavirus pandemic. Who can forget the panic buying that resulted from uncertainty and fear? Remember, no matter what is occurring around you: slow is steady, steady is smooth, and smooth is fast—you will accomplish more by remaining calm under pressure.

No matter what comes your way in life or during your career, stay focused on your upbringing, training, core principles, and beliefs. Recognize that emotion is the enemy of good judgment. Stay true to your ethical North Star. That way, when challenges occur, as they invariably will, you'll always have a safe place to fall back to.

Strive to always stay calm when under pressure.

An F/A-18E Super Hornet mere moments before touchdown and an arrested landing onboard the aircraft carrier, another moment requiring concentration and the ability to stay calm under pressure.

A selfie the author took during a training dogfight with a Japanese Air Self-Defense Force F-4 Phantom II jet, part of the joint U.S.–Japanese Benkyoukai program the author created to improve military cooperation between the two nations.

CHAPTER FOUR

DO THE RIGHT THING, EVEN WHEN NO ONE IS LOOKING

66 No team can succeed unless everyone pulls their own weight. 99

I TIPTOED THROUGH THE doorway, careful not to awaken my wife, Sarah, or our newborn son, Ryan.

It was just after 11 p.m. following a particularly long day at TOPGUN—a red air flight as the "bad guy" in the morning followed by a blue air flight playing the role of "good guy" in the afternoon. The debrief had taken longer than usual, which meant Sarah was already in bed when I finally arrived home.

I made my way to the home office and placed my helmet bag—which held all the briefing materials we needed on every flight—on my office chair. Besides holding our briefing papers, the bag winds up holding everything needed for a flight—gloves, videotapes to record our flight, runway diagrams, snacks, and more. If I need something during a flight, I can usually find it in the bag, zipped securely so nothing will fall out.

Excess stuff builds up over time, so periodically I'd clean out the helmet bag. No one wants to grab hold of a smashed, semi-melted, two-month-old Snickers bar while searching for something more important.

That night, I pulled out some items and then hung my head and sighed. I had accidentally left my briefing cards inside, a rare occurrence as we typically shred them after debriefing the flight.

Aviators use these cards for basic flight info like call signs and radio frequencies. Sometimes, they also include classified information. Today's cards did just that. Having them in my bag—at home—meant that I had inadvertently walked off base without securing all my materials. Luckily, the bag had stayed with me, and I'd driven straight home, so the information was safe. Keeping the cards in my house overnight, however, would be out of the question.

Despite the late hour and the fact that we lived

twenty minutes from base, I had no choice: security procedures required the materials to be secured. I shoved my flight boots back on, cinched up the laces, and hurried to my car to drive back to the base so I could return the materials to the safe and thereby comply with security protocols. I'd be lucky to get back home and into bed before midnight.

Despite the inconvenience and though no one would have been the wiser had I decided to just keep the materials in my house, it was the right thing to do.

Naval aviators are trained in procedural compliance from the first day of flight training. *Following checklists, adhering to time-tested methods, and working within established guidelines are part of what we do to ensure both mission success and safety.* Consistently following the rules also means the men and women with whom I fly can trust me—and trust is critical in the aviation community. In this case, when classified information is involved, proper procedures ensure we're taking the right steps to keep America's secrets protected. Trust me, inquiring minds from other nations *definitely* want to know how we do what we do, as we've repeatedly caught other governments trying to steal our military know-how.

Doing the right thing is also important to me personally. I'd witnessed tragedy during my tour of duty before arriving at TOPGUN while living aboard an aircraft carrier out to sea for deployment—what we typically call a "cruise." Normal day-to-day procedures are important, but some are "lessons written in blood," a rule that exists because someone was seriously injured or killed for not following the correct procedures. Our air wing—a unit comprising all the squadrons onboard the aircraft carrier—experienced such a lesson firsthand.

It was 2004, and I was a junior officer assigned to my very first fighter squadron. I was airborne, circling over the aircraft carrier awaiting my turn to land. It was a crisp, clear night, the kind where every star is easily identifiable. With my night-vision goggles, I could see the aircraft carrier thousands of feet below me, moving steadily along the ocean's surface at twenty-five knots as fighter jets launched into the air from its flight deck.

Do the Right Thing, Even When No One Is Looking

My group of planes would begin landing as soon as all of the airplanes on deck finished launching, a requirement since an aircraft carrier has only one landing area for aircraft.

Soon enough, the launches were complete, and awaiting aircraft began their approach to the carrier. Everything seemed to be flowing smoothly until the radio suddenly crackled to life: "Ninety-nine...delta four, delta four." "Ninety-nine" is a code word that means the carrier was talking to all airplanes then in the sky near the ship. "Delta four" was another code telling us to expect a four-minute delay before we started landing again. Basically, it meant: "Hey everyone, we're on a four-minute delay." This can happen if a landing aircraft blows a tire on hitting the flight deck or if one of the arresting gear wires that catch the planes needs removal and replacement before aircraft can start landing again.

I eased my throttles back to conserve fuel. Good call because before I knew it, the four-minute delay had stretched to eight minutes and then twelve. Two airplanes were now so low on gas they needed to find one of the airborne tankers around the aircraft carrier so they could refuel. I checked my own gauge. I was fine for the moment, but if we delayed much longer I, too, would need fuel.

The radio came alive again, this time ordering us to resume landings. When my turn came, I lined up behind the aircraft carrier to prepare for the approach. Ten minutes later, my wheels touched down, my jet's tailhook caught one of the wires, and I stopped abruptly.

After my jet stopped moving, I looked off to my right to locate the sailor responsible for passing me visual signals, who was standing just to the right side of the landing area. I felt a sharp tug as the wire retracted slightly to pull the jet backward. The sailor then motioned for me to raise my hook to free it from the wire. Taxiing clear of the landing area, I was handed off from sailor to sailor as they positioned me in my assigned parking spot on the ship's flight deck.

Once my jet was parked, I turned off the right engine. After it wound down, I powered down all my avionics—radar system, radios, and the other aircraft systems that we normally use in flight. Satisfied that

Do the Right Thing, Even When No One Is Looking

I had completed all steps on my shutdown checklist, I turned off the left engine, opening the cockpit's canopy as I did so.

I hadn't thought much about the reason for the earlier delay. I just grabbed my helmet bag, gave my aircraft a quick once-over, thanked the sailors on the flight deck, and headed into the ship to make my way back to the ready room where squadron pilots congregate. The atmosphere there was somber.

I took off my helmet and put it in my assigned chair along with my bag. Turning to another pilot while pulling out my earplugs, I asked, "Hey, what's going on? Why the long faces?"

My friend sadly shook his head before saying, "A sailor died tonight. He was in the hangar bay, walking in between an S-3 Viking refueling jet and the wall when the ship started to turn. Whoever chained down the S-3 hadn't tightened the chains completely, so the jet rolled forward as the ship turned, crushing and killing him. It was gruesome."

I shuddered. For safety reasons, aircraft are always "chocked and chained" when parked onboard the aircraft carrier. Sailors place chocks both in front of and behind the wheels and then use multiple heavy chains to securely fasten the jet and keep it from moving. Unlike airports, aircraft carriers are constantly moving. They bob up and down with the waves, roll from side to side when the ship turns, and lurch in every other direction you can think of. If an aircraft isn't properly chained down, it can roll out of position, crushing equipment and hurting anyone who happens to be nearby.

That's exactly what had happened here. It was a tragedy of epic proportions—more so because this sailor's death had been entirely preventable. His life would have been saved if the sailor in charge of properly securing the plane hadn't left too much slack in the chains—a seemingly simple action that occurs hundreds of times every day while operating at sea.

You never know how doing the basics of your job incorrectly can have a major impact on someone else's life. A sailor had died needlessly due to carelessness—the same reason I'd nearly been killed years before when a mechanic left a rag in my jet's engine.

Experiencing these two incidents early in my career

reinforced to me the importance of personal integrity. Someone else shouldn't have to hold us accountable to a higher standard to ensure the job is done right. Successful teams are always built on trust—and trust requires everyone to complete their assigned tasks properly, every time, no matter how insignificant they might seem. No team can succeed unless everyone pulls their own weight.

Your actions always speak louder than your words ever can. Those around you—your friends, family, neighbors, other students, or coworkers—are counting on you to do your best. When faced with adversity—or worse, the opportunity to take shortcuts—commit to doing the harder right thing rather than the sometimes easier wrong thing. Who among us (myself included) has walked by a piece of trash without stopping to pick it up? Taking the time to stop and do the small things correctly becomes a lifelong habit, one that positively impacts everyone around you, just as we benefit when others do the same for us.

Remember to **do the right thing, even when no one is looking**.

F/A-18 Super Hornets parked on the aft end of USS *Ronald Reagan* (CVN 73) flight deck while sailing in formation with U.S. and Japanese warships in the Sea of Japan in 2016.

CHAPTER FIVE

ANTICIPATE PROBLEMS

❝ In real life, perspiration trumps
inspiration nine times out of ten… ❞

SOMETIMES, THROUGH OUR TOPGUN work, we enjoyed rare opportunities. In 2007, a British Broadcasting Company (BBC) television crew visited us in Fallon, Nevada.

The producers asked me to appear in an episode for *Horizon*, a science and philosophy show that is one of Britain's longest-running series. The episode's premise was straightforward and also served as its title: "How to Make Better Decisions."

The producers were exploring a theory called precognition, the ability of some highly trained members of specific career fields to see into the future. The question the producers sought to answer was this: Were

TOPGUN instructors so successful because our intensive training had prepared us to instinctively know what our adversaries would do before they did it?

The BBC crew arrived in late summer to record video and conduct interviews with a few of us. Our opinion was unanimous: no, precognition doesn't exist for aircrew. Like everyone else, we can't know for certain what will happen in the future. Few TOPGUN instructors look anything like Tom Cruise, and none of us can read minds.

On the flip side, our high levels of practice and study have equipped us well to predict combat outcomes. Even though the fighter jets we fly and the adversaries we face travel in three-dimensional space, the number of options available to any given pilot at any given time is finite.

As a dogfight progresses, a jet's airspeed typically slows, and the choices available to a pilot rapidly decrease. A slow-moving adversary can either fly their aircraft level across the horizon or descend, since the aircraft doesn't have the airspeed needed to gain altitude. Similarly, if its altitude is very low, then it can either stay level to the horizon or fly higher because going lower would cause them to crash into the ground.

Anticipate Problems

Aviators use this knowledge to box in their adversaries, "driving" them into a position where they will lose. With thousands of hours of study and practice, fighter pilots can predict likely outcomes and plan their next moves accordingly so as to achieve that result. Author Malcolm Gladwell theorizes that mastering a skill requires ten thousand hours of practice. If those hours were put back-to-back, they would total nearly fourteen months. We put in those hours and then some. Our abilities as fighter pilots stem from our extensive preparation, rather than precognition, though admittedly, the latter may sound more exciting. Knowing what to expect depends far more on a pilot's experience, practice, and training. In real life, perspiration trumps inspiration nine times out of ten, and every student attending TOP-GUN already has years of practice before they arrive.

While the episode was being shot, I was reminded that these skills had saved my life more than once during my previous fleet tour; one incident stood out.

In 2004, my squadron was deployed onboard the nuclear-powered aircraft carrier USS *George Washington*, from which we launched daily missions into Iraq while patrolling the Persian Gulf. We'd been at sea for four months in the Gulf when I was asked to go on a special mission to help train members of the Jordanian air force, one of our long-standing partners in the Middle East. Excited to see a new country and eager for a chance to go ashore, I accepted.

Within a few weeks, we had packed our equipment into five F/A-18 Hornets. Launching from the *George Washington*, we flew first into Kuwait and Iraq before turning northwest to enter Jordan and land at an air base in Azraq, a remote town with a population of ten thousand located about an hour east of Amman, Jordan's capital city. Here, we'd have the opportunity to practice missions with supersonic Jordanian F-16 Viper and Mirage F1 fighter jets.

The experience was all I had hoped for. We dined with Jordanian pilots, learned Eastern Arabic numerals (so we could read the numbers painted on their jets), and soaked up the culture. We also flew numerous practice missions with the Jordanians, a valuable experience during my first tour of duty.

During my second week in Azraq, I was scheduled to

Anticipate Problems

dogfight against a Jordanian F-16. I was looking forward to the flight. Smaller and lighter than my F/A-18C Hornet, the F-16 is a nimble aircraft and can easily reach supersonic speeds—so it would be an exciting matchup. The Jordanian fighter pilot hosted me at his squadron's headquarters and provided breakfast before we briefed, an incredible show of hospitality.

With our coordination and flight brief complete, we split up to go our separate ways: I to my F/A-18C parked on the flight line and he to his F-16, which was located in an underground bunker. His need to park his jet in an underground bunker was a stark reminder of the state of affairs in the Middle East, where conflict between neighboring nations is not unusual.

Soon, both our jets were airborne, and we headed to our assigned "working area," a section of airspace reserved exclusively for us, which minimized the chances that a wayward airliner or other military aircraft would intrude. I expected a straightforward flight.

Unfortunately, I was proved wrong during our very first engagement.

We were conducting preplanned, high-aspect

dogfighting, starting about twenty miles apart. This allowed each of us to use our fighter jet's radar to locate the other plane and track it as we flew closer to one another. Once inside five miles, we'd be able to see each other using our eyes (a "visual" pickup), allowing us to fly past each other, at which point we'd start the fight.

There was only one problem: as our aircraft approached each other, I could see his jet…but he couldn't see mine.

And I had no idea.

This meant I was following my routine training, pointing my jet toward his so that I'd pass him just beyond his right side. As I did so, I noticed his jet's nose continued to point directly at mine. Odd and surprisingly aggressive.

At this point, we were only a mile and a half from each other and closing fast, so I maneuvered my aircraft in an attempt to keep a safe distance between us as we passed one another.

Once again, his jet's nose continued to point straight at mine. Something was wrong. If nothing changed, our aircraft would collide in less than three seconds, likely killing us both and causing a massive fireball in the sky that would rain pieces of our aircraft down on the desert sands below. I had to do something immediately.

The only option remaining was an extremely hard pull up and to the left. I hoped that this would move me far enough out of the way that we'd avoid colliding while allowing me to keep my eyes on what his airplane was doing.

In the blink of an eye, our jets roared past each other, separated by only a few feet. We were so close, I actually heard and felt his jet engine's exhaust inside my *own* aircraft.

I could tell that our near collision had shocked him, as his aircraft belatedly jerked away from mine, maneuvering in what we call a "basic fighter maneuvers error," meaning that his first move had put him in bad fighting position.

After a few minutes of continued fighting, I emerged victorious but badly shaken. I'd had my share of eye-opening in-flight emergencies, but this was the first time another plane had nearly collided with mine.

After landing, I learned what had happened.

The Jordanian pilot had found me with his radar and used this info to point his jet toward my location. Since my fighter was painted gray, the color of the sky behind me, he never saw my aircraft. He just kept pointing toward where his radar was telling him to go in the hope that he'd eventually find me. Since our flight plan had called for us to pass each other at close range, I didn't know until the last moment that he didn't see me.

It was a crucial wake-up call regarding what would become one of my most important lessons: anticipate problems. We emerged unscathed only because I had been lucky enough to see him and because I had made a proactive maneuver to avoid a collision rather than assume he'd safely avoid hitting me. Otherwise, we would have been toast.

I had failed to anticipate problems that might arise when flying with pilots from another nation. Heck, even pilots from other branches of the U.S. armed forces have different standards for conducting training flights. I could have avoided this incident altogether had I thoughtfully considered issues that might arise during our flight and then addressed them during our preflight planning or during the flight brief.

Years later, as a squadron commander in Japan, I always made sure to work with my team to plan twelve months in advance. We war-gamed likely outcomes to ensure that we were being proactive, not reactive, with major decisions. This would allow the squadron team to make informed decisions instead of being continually surprised by events as they occurred. Taking a proactive approach to everything turned the squadron around. We became the top-ranked squadron out of the eight on the carrier, and by the end of my tenure, we had risen to the top of all Navy F/A-18 squadrons in the Western Hemisphere (out of twenty), earning the coveted Battle Efficiency Award.

The same lesson paid dividends during my hitch in a very different role in 2017, when I served as director of communications and chief speechwriter for Secretary of Defense James Mattis. I worked with my team to identify all the major events that we expected to come our way during the year ahead. When we experienced a rare break in our busy schedules, we would begin planning events for months down the road to gain a head start, anticipating that we would be far busier by then. When we traveled overseas, we brainstormed likely outcomes and planned accordingly.

Planning for success can be as easy as printing the next twelve months of your calendar to anticipate what's coming down the road. Or it can be as simple as writing your next day's schedule on a piece of paper the night before so that you'll be prepared. A student can look ahead at course schedules to predict periods of high stress and use those predictions to balance out their workload. A barista, knowing that the morning rush always puts the team behind, can prepare some heavily used items the night prior. A manager responsible for conducting performance evaluations can chart these on the calendar in advance and can jot down quick weekly notes so that, when it comes time to sit down and discuss ways to improve, he or she can offer more insightful comments.

Also, think deeply about your decisions. If you're thinking of leaving one job for another, consider the likely outcomes beyond just a boost in your pay. Will you have to move? What is the new team like? How will this one decision affect the many other aspects of your life? How will this choice impact the next two or three decisions that will invariably follow (often referred to as "second-" and "third-order effects")? ***Thinking further down the road will help ensure that you're not caught by surprise.*** As President Dwight D. Eisenhower said, "Plans are worthless, but planning is indispensable." Learning to anticipate problems and then creating plans for success is a lifelong skill.

You never know what life will bring your way. We may not be able to see into the future, but we can tip the scales in our favor by being proactive rather than reactive. Learn to create your own success. As Branch Rickey, the Brooklyn Dodgers general manager who signed Jackie Robinson in 1945, liked to say, "Luck is the residue of design." We always have a vote in the final outcome.

Anticipate problems to give yourself the best chance of success.

The author in a F/A-18E Super Hornet shortly after taxiing onto the runway to take off from Naval Air Facility Atsugi, a joint Japanese–U.S. air base approximately twenty-four miles southwest of Tokyo.

CHAPTER SIX

DON'T CONFUSE ACTIVITY WITH PROGRESS

❝ Volume of work doesn't equal quality of work. ❞

ANY TOPGUN INSTRUCTOR leads a life marked by perpetual motion.

Our daily routine meant we started early, arriving at the office before 6 a.m. to prepare for our first flight brief or lecture. We didn't leave until our last flight had been debriefed and the grade sheet completed, usually after 10 p.m. Time was so precious that we commonly found ourselves feasting on a "fighter pilot's breakfast"—a Snickers bar washed down with a can of soda—and most days we barely carved out time for lunch before dashing off to the next event. Throughout the day there were the usual emails, meetings, and phone calls associated with our job.

Our frenetic pace usually required putting in a full day of work on Saturday to catch up on paperwork or to prepare for the next week's agenda—or both. If we were murderboarding, we were probably grinding it out for part of Sunday, too, which gave us little or no time off during the week.

We were also frequently on the road, teaching students during training detachments at another air base, developing our own tactics, or working alongside instructors from the U.S. Air Force, Navy SEALs, or the intelligence community.

I was lucky—my wife, Sarah, had a job as a graphic designer supporting TOPGUN, which meant she and I worked in the same building. It was a good thing, too. She saw me far more frequently at work than at home, and even that wasn't often.

The long hours and heavy travel schedule made it necessary for instructors to be effective and efficient with our time. We couldn't waste a second. If we frittered away our time, things piled up. As a relatively small, nimble staff with significant responsibilities, everyone had to carry their load.

Don't Confuse Activity with Progress

Which brings us to a related—and often underappreciated—skill: prioritizing. With so many tasks competing for our time, we needed to sift through the to-do list to tackle both the "quick kills" as well as those deemed most important. A quick interaction with another instructor helped teach me how best to employ my time.

She was a senior instructor on the TOPGUN staff. Catching me in the hallway as I discussed the number of tasks on my plate, she offered to pass along a few pointers before waving me to follow her into one of the briefing rooms. Grabbing a marker, she marched up to the whiteboard and drew a huge square. Inside that square she drew a large plus sign, creating two columns and two rows.

To the left of the top row she wrote the word "important." Below it, to the left of the second row, she wrote "not important." Moving to the top of the chart, she wrote "urgent" above the left column and then "not urgent" above the right one.

Glancing at me, she pointed to the upper left box and said, "This represents the items you need to do that are both urgent *and* important, which means you should complete them immediately."

Pointing to the upper right box, she said, "These items are important but not urgent, so you have time to think about them and conduct some planning."

She moved her finger to the lower left box saying, "These are the items that are urgent but not important. Be careful with these, as you can waste your time doing frivolous things."

The final box, the one to the lower right, was for items both unimportant and not urgent, which could be discarded completely. Avoid those at all costs.

	Urgent	Not Urgent
Important	Complete Immediately	Plan These
Not Important	Danger: Frivolous	Don't Waste Your Time

Don't Confuse Activity with Progress

This was the first time I'd heard of using this technique for prioritizing my to-do items, and it stuck. She later told me that it was actually one of author Stephen Covey's *7 Habits of Highly Effective People* (Simon & Schuster, 1990). Covey had popularized an idea highlighted by President Dwight D. Eisenhower in a 1954 speech to the Second Assembly of the World Council of Churches. In the speech, Eisenhower quoted Dr. J. Roscoe Miller, president of Northwestern University, who had said, "I have two kinds of problems, the urgent and the important. The urgent are not important, and the important are never urgent."

The ability to organize one's life according to what has become known as the "Eisenhower Principle" requires that we understand the difference between what is urgent and what is important.

I'd see this principle put to the test a few years later when I left my fighter jet cockpit to go fly a desk at the Pentagon for a couple of years. Working there revealed the other side of the coin—people getting burned out in their job, typically owing to the arbitrarily long hours. TOPGUN had been difficult, but the continual change of missions kept things fresh, a much harder goal to achieve when working in a cubicle farm.

I was serving as the speechwriter for the most senior military leader in the U.S. Navy, the chief of naval operations. This is a person who rose through the ranks to become a four-star admiral. In many cases, this takes close to four decades. Although the title is unique, each of the armed forces—Army, Navy, Air Force, Marine Corps, and, now, the Space Force—has its own four-star admiral or general at the helm.

Any large bureaucracy requires a proportionately sizeable administrative and management function to ensure that thousands of tasks are handled swiftly and efficiently. But staffs have a way of taking on lives of their own. They expand steadily over time, and the Pentagon was no exception. The sheer number of people working there was staggering. Most publicly available sources put the number of Pentagon employees at over twenty-three thousand and growing.

In fact, Parkinson's law—created by a career civil servant in Britain—puts forward a mathematical formula to determine how quickly large organizations

Don't Confuse Activity with Progress

grow simply because they exist in the first place (spoiler alert: it's five to seven percent per year, on average). I like two corollaries of Parkinson's law:

1. If you wait until the last minute... it only takes a minute.
2. Work expands to fill the time available for its completion.

These incredibly large Pentagon staffs each had different roles and responsibilities. Some people were extremely busy, while others finished most of their day's work by 11 a.m.—but whether you were a worker bee or a drone, you were expected to be at your desk for long hours.

I felt lucky, as my boss tended to be judicious with his time, trying hard to maintain a consistent 7:30 a.m. to 5 p.m. office schedule. Some leaders, however, believed the appearance of hard work—putting in long, grueling hours—meant more than results. That kind of attitude drives morale into the basement.

If you've ever had this type of boss, you probably

know what I mean: if they're in the office, then you're in the office. I knew from my time at TOPGUN the importance of focusing on outcomes to achieve the best results, not an indiscriminately long workday spent at your desk twiddling your thumbs just to put in the appearance of working long hours.

Leaders set the tone for their organizations. And each leader gets a choice. When I returned to Japan to lead a fighter squadron after my time at TOPGUN, I expected high-quality work from my sailors, but I also let them know that when their job was done, it was time to go home. In fact, I told the men and women under my command that I wanted each of them to be both lazy and selfish. Lazy, in that they needed to create the best possible results with the least amount of effort. And selfish, knowing that it's critical to make time to reflect and create a plan of attack so they could be more deliberate with their actions.

Volume of work doesn't equal quality of work. Fixating solely on quantity burns out your team and lowers morale. Leaders need to provide opportunities for their teams to work efficiently ("Work smarter, not harder")

Don't Confuse Activity with Progress

so they can recharge their batteries. That way, there's always a reserve to tap into when you most need it. You can't floor it when you're on empty.

This is also an important lesson for anyone starting out in the workforce or taking on a new job: don't put artificially high pressure on yourself to outdo the boss's long hours on the job. If you find yourself coming in far too early or leaving much too late, ask yourself one question: Are you doing it because your job requires it or because you're *assuming* you should do so? The desire to impress the boss who just hired you can lead to decisions that cause premature burnout—and when that happens, neither you nor your boss nor the organization succeeds.

Find a consistent pace that works for you and your team. Focus your time on those items that are urgent and important—and avoid those that are just distractions.

To maximize your performance while maintaining your stamina, ***don't confuse activity with progress***.

The men and women who made up the "Dambusters" of Strike Fighter Squadron ONE NINE FIVE onboard the USS *Ronald Reagan* during the summer of 2016. The author, serving as the squadron's commanding officer, is front and center.

CHAPTER SEVEN

NEVER WAIT TO MAKE A DIFFERENCE

> 66 Your probability of success is zero
> when you don't take the shot. 99

A UNIQUE ASPECT OF TOPGUN is that its staff is run collectively by its junior officers, not by any senior military leader.

Normally, the U.S. military is rigidly hierarchical. Each unit has its version of a commanding officer, typically a senior officer who determines the organization's agenda while supervising day-to-day operations.

A typical U.S. Navy strike fighter squadron is a good example. A squadron is generally composed of around 220 sailors—both officers and enlisted—with the commanding officer standing alone at the top of the pyramid. He or she is assisted by a second-in-command, the executive officer, and a command master chief—the most senior enlisted person on the team. You then have additional layers, starting with department heads who oversee primary squadron functions such as operations, maintenance, and administration. Under the department heads are junior officers and senior enlisted leadership in charge of divisions composed of rank-and-file sailors who handle more specialized functions: engine maintenance, upkeep of an aircraft's electronic systems, personnel support, and many more. The commanding officer's instructions and decisions trickle down into the organization's lower echelons, while reports and feedback make their way back up.

This type of hierarchy is found in every branch of the armed forces. The only difference is the seniority of the ranking officer and the size of the command.

Not so at TOPGUN, which still operates more like a startup than the fifty-one-year-old organization that it is—let alone as part of the U.S. Navy, which was founded during the Revolutionary War.

Instead of a commanding officer laying out everything, junior officers set priorities, maintain TOPGUN's professional standards, and direct day-to-day operations. The staff, however, does have two primary leaders, both junior officers, who work together: the training officer and the standardization officer.

The training officer—typically one of the longest-serving instructors on the team—serves as its de facto senior leader, guiding strategy, shaping the program's schedule, and making high-level decisions regarding the staff's function. The training officer also handles staff development and job assignments, providing instructors with opportunities for personal and professional growth.

The standardization officer, or Stan-O, is another long-serving instructor responsible for assigning lectures to junior staff members, setting the murderboard schedule, and maintaining TOPGUN's institutional memory about how major decisions regarding fleet tactics were made. The Stan-O is also responsible for enforcing fines for infractions committed by staff members: for example, one dollar for every minute late to a meeting, payments for filing grade sheets late, or—my favorite—five dollars for any quote from the movie *Top Gun*.

TOPGUN'S TOP 10

The Standardization Board—akin to a company's board of directors—is composed of the ten longest-serving junior officers on the staff, regardless of rank. They alone are responsible for high-level decision making. While all instructors attend Standardization Board meetings, only board members have the authority to vote on whether to approve new tactical recommendations for the half-million members of the U.S. Navy and Marine Corps. The "Stan Board" considers current tactics, any updated threats posed by changes in a foreign nation's capabilities—new fighter jets, air- and surface-launched missiles, tactics, and more. The Stan Board then decides whether the proposed changes are necessary before deciding to implement updates with such potentially far-reaching consequences.

As mentioned, every instructor is responsible for carrying out daily tasks: training students, mastering the subject material they teach, and representing TOPGUN to outside organizations, to name a few. As members of a professional organization, the instructors' most sacred role is to uphold standards: for themselves, the students, and the institution as a whole. If

A sailor signaling that an F/A-18 is ready for takeoff. There's no room for shrinking violets on the flight deck. Sailors are expected to speak up if they see an unsafe situation developing.

something's not quite right, they are to identify it and fix it on the spot instead of waiting for someone else to weigh in.

Like other squadrons, TOPGUN has a commanding officer called a "department head," a senior Navy commander who was recently in charge of a frontline fleet squadron. This officer—typically an ex-TOPGUN instructor—serves as a mentor, providing experience and perspective to the junior officers. He or she also represents the team at meetings with senior military organizations.

The best commanding officers lead by example: going through the murderboard process, teaching a lecture, and becoming qualified to instruct students during training flights. In short, while the commanding officer is an important part of the organization, this person is mostly responsible for running interference so the staff can remain focused on the task at hand: producing world-class aviators. TOPGUN also has a de facto executive officer—also typically a former instructor—who assists the commanding officer with external meetings and relationships with other organizations.

Never Wait to Make a Difference

During my two and a half years as an instructor, I appreciated how "flat" our organization was, that is, how nonhierarchical. In public, we certainly respected any differences in rank, offering the proper "sir" or "ma'am" when appropriate. But behind closed doors we were peers—and everyone had an equal voice. *We knew that an organization's most senior person doesn't have a monopoly on good ideas,* so it was important to hear from the experts on any given topic, regardless of their rank.

In other military units, when a junior person asks why we do something a certain way, the answer generally lies somewhere between "because I told you to" and "because that's how we've always done it." A more colorful response is to tell junior personnel to simply "shut up and color," a directive to stop offering suggestions and simply focus on the task at hand (like telling a child to be quiet and color in their coloring book). And there's always the "leader" who's known for telling a subordinate, "If I wanted your opinion, I'd give it to you."

While sometimes such remarks are delivered in an offhanded or tongue-in-cheek manner, the typical result can be damaging: junior personnel learn to keep their good ideas and their questions to themselves. Unfortunately, it's altogether too easy for this type of culture to permeate an organization, leading personnel at all ranks to believe that the way to advance is to do their best at their assigned task, and not much more.

The overall result is that, while the military is generally very good at maintaining the status quo, it is much slower to embrace new technology or to respond to changing world events.

The way TOPGUN is organized, however, enabled us to avoid the intellectual stagnation that marks many military commands. We were actively encouraged to challenge the status quo, ensuring we always stayed at least one step ahead of our adversaries or those who would seek to challenge America in combat. Bruising someone's ego was permissible. Losing in combat was not. So any impediment to innovation and effectiveness went by the wayside.

During my time as a TOPGUN instructor, I was a lieutenant—a very junior officer—as were most of the others on the staff. Being afforded such tremendous responsibility as a junior officer allowed me to feel comfortable in pushing for substantive change throughout my career, even after I left TOPGUN.

During a two-decade career of direct observation and conversation, I watched many people—from the most junior sailor to senior admirals to corporate leaders—hesitate to act on great ideas because they elected to wait for some arbitrary moment of opportunity that never came.

One junior sailor told me he'd created a system for organizing paperwork that saved the Navy thousands of dollars per year, but he waited two years to unveil it because he didn't want to be seen as the new guy trying to show off. Another time, I had lunch with a Navy captain in the Pentagon who had devised a terrific plan for helping families get the support they need while moving across the country. Unfortunately, he felt he couldn't suggest it until he became an admiral. He never made admiral and retired instead, taking his good idea with him.

These are just two small examples from among the hundreds of great ideas I've heard from service members with whom I had the pleasure of working. Most of their concepts were never realized. In nearly every case, they felt they had to attain some arbitrary higher rank before they would be in a position to implement the changes needed. In some cases, they were simply afraid to fail. In most cases, the rank they were shooting for never arrived.

No matter what type of job you have, you may feel it is difficult to rock the boat when you're a part of a large, top-down organization. It may seem that there are too few reasons to try something new and a million reasons not too.

But if I've learned one thing, it's that nothing in life is ever guaranteed. Waiting until the perfect moment to act could mean you never act. As fighter pilots say, "Your probability of success is zero when you don't take the shot." Success is achieved by taking calculated risks.

Develop the courage to make daring, significant impacts at every stage of your life and career. The reality is that courage and self-confidence are very much like muscles—they feel uncomfortable when you first start using them, but they always grow stronger over time.

Remember, fortune favors the bold. It's hard to reap rewards without ever taking risks, so ***never wait to make a difference***.

The author landing aboard the USS *Ronald Reagan* for his last "trap" (arrested landing) as a U.S. Navy fighter pilot in 2016.

CHAPTER EIGHT

ALWAYS HAVE A WINGMAN

66 Fly alone. Die alone. **99**

IN THE ORIGINAL *Top Gun* movie, a dogfight depicts four TOPGUN students—Maverick and Goose in one jet, Hollywood and Wolfman in another—going head-to-head with two of the toughest senior instructors on the staff: Viper and Jester.

Everything starts off just fine, as the students move in for the kill behind the two instructors. It even looks like the fight could be over quickly, but Viper and Jester split up, their aircraft flying in separate directions. They have cleverly designed a trap to pull Maverick away from his flight lead—Hollywood—which would leave both Maverick and Hollywood exposed and vulnerable.

Maverick is smart at first. He follows his training

and does the right thing, staying with Hollywood to provide cover as they both fight Jester. This is the quickest way to win: once they defeat Jester, they can go on together to fight Viper.

But Maverick gets greedy. He knows Viper is the biggest and toughest instructor. Taking him down would be a significant victory—and *he* wants the glory. When Goose sees Viper's aircraft off in the distance, Maverick goes for the gold. Abandoning Hollywood, Maverick peels off to pursue Viper in one-on-one combat.

The end result? Hollywood is defeated, and with Viper serving as a decoy from the start, Jester swings in to kill Maverick from behind. He and Goose never saw Jester coming. Maverick's self-indulgence transformed what might have been a sure win into two defeats.

Back on the ground, the defeated students—Maverick, Goose, Hollywood, and Wolfman—are sulking in their locker room contemplating their loss as Jester walks in, still wearing his flight gear. Jester might have strolled in—cocky and gloating—after winning. But that's not how he feels at all.

He's *furious*.

Always Have a Wingman

Storming over to Maverick, he snarls: "That was some of the best flying I've seen yet. Right up to the part where you got killed. You never, *ever* leave your wingman." (Both men and women are referred to as "wingmen," a gender-neutral term that identifies an aircraft's position in formation.)

There's a reason why the actual TOPGUN instructors consulting on the movie insisted on this scene being included: it accurately reflects real combat. When you fly the skies alone and unafraid, bad things can—and do—happen. Why? Because there's no one there to check your "6 o'clock"—the position directly behind you.

I learned that the hard way as a TOPGUN student.

We were on a type of mission known as a "division self-escort strike." *Division* is the Navy's term for four aircraft operating together. In a self-escort strike, the blue air have to fight their way to the target against the red air, drop their bombs, defend against any simulated ground-launched missiles, and then fight their way back out against any remaining aircraft that might decide to challenge them. It is one of the most complicated and difficult types of missions because it forces pilots to exercise every skill in one flight.

It is also an absolute blast.

On this particular day, we were flying at 27,000 feet, clicking right along at about 550 miles per hour. I was in one of four aircraft headed inbound to drop bombs onto a series of old tanks used for target practice in a training range known as B-17, or "Bravo 17."

For today's mission, I was assigned the far-left side of our flight's formation. This meant that when I looked out the right side of my jet—what we call the "3 o'clock position"—I could see the other aircraft lined up into the distance. We were all spread out from one another, a formation that provides two benefits. First, it makes it difficult for the red air to spot all of us at once. Even after finding one jet, they still had to look for—and find—three others, a much more difficult task when their targets are all separated. Second, having distance between us allowed us to focus on our radars and other information systems. We couldn't have done that if we had been flying only a few feet from one another, since our attention would have been focused on staying in position to prevent a collision.

Our radars scanned for enemy fighters as we headed west toward the target. I kept my head down, scanning both my radar's display as well as the situational display—a map on a separate screen showing where other airplanes, ground threats, and targets were located. It was critical that we watch our radar screens because we were flying over mountainous terrain, with peaks reaching over 8,700 feet. This should have been our first warning.

Radar signals are blocked by physical objects. If I'm scanning for an airliner, life is good because there's nothing but air between my jet and the airliner. My radar signal will reflect off the airliner's metal skin, return to my jet, and show up as a contact on my radar screen.

But mountainous terrain makes everything tricky. Shrewd red air pilots will fly at low altitudes next to the mountains, knowing they are hidden from our radars. Then, when they spot us flying overhead, they can ascend, sneak up behind us, and take their best shot.

In many cases, the blue air pilots never see them. It's an incredibly effective maneuver—and it's how I was nearly shot during this training flight.

Not seeing anything on my radar screen, I began ticking through my checklist to switch over to air-to-ground mode in preparation for dropping my bombs. That's when my helmet's earphones came alive: "HUNTER 1-4, BREAK RIGHT...BOGEY AT YOUR 5 O'CLOCK, ONE MILE!" a frantic call indicating that an unknown aircraft—a "bogey," World War II–era slang for an unknown contact—had popped up one mile behind me and slightly off to the right.

I slammed my control stick to the right, popped some flares, and began descending in an aggressive, high-G, slicing turn while desperately scanning the sky for enemy aircraft. The hunter had become the hunted. And I didn't like it one bit. *Where was my adversary?* I saw nothing. But the wingman to my right side did—and made a hard turn to engage him.

There! As I turned, I finally spotted the bogey following me. Good news: I had spotted him. Horrible news: he was on my tail. Luckily, my turn allowed my wingman to gain the advantage quickly. A few seconds later, I got the radio call that I was dying to hear: "Kill bandit in a right-hand turn." My wingman had saved my bacon.

This impromptu dogfight required the four of us to return our jets into a formation, and in short order we were over the target and had sent our bombs hurtling toward the ground. Mission success.

This lesson plays out over and over again throughout any aviator's career. ***Those who fly with a wingman are far more likely to survive. Those without are at the mercy of fate, and those odds aren't in your favor.***

Fly alone. Die alone.

During my twenty-year career in the Navy, wingmen rescued me from a midair collision over Iraq, helped during in-flight emergencies, and spoke for me when my radios failed—all ensuring that I arrived safely home each night. We also had each other's back outside the cockpit, offering support during particularly tough projects or passing along helpful tips during challenging times. A wingman can help a pilot see around corners, anticipate problems, and create solutions far better than anything we could ever come up with on our own.

This lesson was reinforced daily while I worked for Secretary Mattis in the Pentagon. America's military has global responsibilities—and those responsibilities exist 24 hours a day, 7 days a week, 365 days a year. With so much information flying about and so many leaders involved, no single person could ever hope to fully grasp all the details in play. It was invaluable to me when a coworker stopped by after a meeting to say, "I was just in a meeting with Mattis, and he said we're changing our force levels in the Middle East" or "We've just made a decision regarding the use of global cyber operations." Having wingmen throughout the Pentagon helped ensure I could do my job to the best of my abilities and ensured that Mattis and the rest of the team had the most up-to-date information. I would have undoubtedly failed in my job had I not had so many others providing insight and assistance.

No matter what job you may have, you will need outside help if you want to experience long-term success. Develop a close network of trusted friends who will watch your 6 o'clock, who will always be there when you need them most, and who aren't afraid to tell you when you're about to do something that compromises your values. ***Friends who are willing to tell you what you need to hear—and not necessarily what you want to hear—are worth their weight in gold.***

Develop professional relationships in the workplace. Find coworkers you trust to tell you the truth—and do the same for them. Support each other and don't hesitate to jump in and assist when you see someone struggling with their workload. They'll appreciate your help, and you'll have contributed to building goodwill and a positive team environment.

When the going gets tough, ***always have a wingman***.

The author conducting a flight briefing while serving as a department head in Strike Fighter Squadron ONE ZERO TWO during his first tour of duty to Japan in 2008.

CHAPTER NINE

PUT THE BOTTOM LINE UP FRONT

> 66 Learn to communicate the most important messages early—and often… 99

Firmly holding my ruler against the whiteboard, I drew four long black lines connecting three black circles, a black box, and a red triangle.

It was today's strike route.

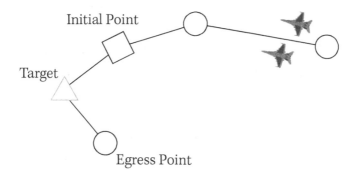

The line connecting the first two black circles represented points we'd fly to as we advanced toward our target. Next came the black box, our "initial point," where we'd make our final turn toward the target area for a bombing run. The initial point also marked the location where we'd shift our attention from aerial combat to preparing for the bombing run. The red triangle on the whiteboard indicated our objective: two old aircraft parked in the middle of a runway (Bravo-17) located in the middle of the desert, 270 miles northwest of Las Vegas. The last line went from the target to the third circle—our "egress point," the place we'd head to for safety once off target.

I had just put my finishing touches on the board when my instructor walked in. Nodding appreciatively at what passed for my artwork, he slung himself onto the couch. He would be my wingman for today's event.

Three minutes to go.

At the top of the hour, I started my brief.

"Aaaand, hack," I said, "the time is zero-seven hundred. Today's mission is a self-escort strike into Bravo-17 to destroy two aircraft parked on the runway's east side. We've observed enemy coastal air patrols along our strike route, so we can expect to fight our way in—and we might have to fight our way back out, too. Big picture: these aircraft *must* be destroyed, so we are willing to accept a high level of risk during today's mission. If for any reason we get separated or one of us goes down, the other will continue to the target to destroy their assigned aircraft."

My poker-faced instructor scribbled some notes on his clipboard. TOPGUN instructors always take pages of notes to support the debrief. It's part of our charm.

I continued, walking him through the specifics of the mission: radio frequencies we'd use during the flight, specifics about our strike route, and, of course, the targets themselves. I dove into detail on today's expected red air threat—Russian-made MiG-29s (being simulated by other F/A-18s). Our only break was that the expected surface-to-air missile threat near the targets was assessed as minimal.

Briefing complete, we headed to the flight line, fired up the jets, and were airborne about an hour later.

It wasn't long before we made the customary radio

Sailors standing to the right of catapult three on USS *Carl Vinson*'s flight deck. The flight deck is awash with the sounds of jet noise and public announcements, requiring sailors to put the bottom line up front because time is a precious commodity.

calls: "Red air set west," signifying that they were in position and ready to begin. We replied in kind: "Roger. Check tapes on, fight's on," a call officially starting the fight while reminding my wingman to turn on his video recorder. Without video, we can't debrief the flight— resulting in an automatic "refly" to do it all over again the next day, regardless of our performance.

I'd briefed my instructor to automatically deploy, so he was already moving his jet off to my left side as he created some distance between us. We were both busy in our cockpits: scanning the radar display, looking for white streaks of contrails or any other signs of bad guys, and scanning behind each other's jet to see whether someone was trying to sneak up behind us.

Our mission's schedule contained an inflexible moment known as "time on target," when our bombs needed to hit the target. Arriving early? Pull the throttles back a little to decrease airspeed. On track to arrive too late? Nudge the throttles forward a bit.

It wasn't long before we had our first customers: two simulated MiG-29 Fulcrums were headed our way.

My instructor took a shot. I still wasn't seeing

anything on my radar, so after a moment my instructor took a second shot to ensure each bad guy had a missile heading their way. At the last moment, a contact popped up on my radar screen, but I wasn't able to take a shot before the four of us were passing each other at the merge: my flight heading west and the enemy red air heading east.

One of the bad guys was rocking his wings, an acknowledgment that he had "died" from one of the missile shots. The other red air, however, was very much alive and turning back aggressively toward us. I turned to engage.

The remaining enemy pilot was good. Very good. It took far too long to complete the dogfight. A window of opportunity opened just long enough for me to squeeze the trigger to fire a simulated AIM-120 missile that allowed me to claim the kill. I breathed a sigh of relief. On with the mission.

Only one thing was missing: my wingman. Somewhere during the fight we'd lost sight of each other. I glanced down at my situational display, which showed he was about six miles in front of me. Checking my clock told me what I'd instinctively known: my extended dog-fight meant I wouldn't reach the target in time—but my wingman would. He'd done as I instructed back at the brief: "If for any reason we get separated or one of us goes down, the other will continue to the target to destroy their assigned aircraft."

I trailed along behind him, mindful to remain outside the range of any surface-to-air missiles. I monitored my radios, checked my radar for any additional contacts, and headed to the point I knew he'd fly to once he was off target.

A few minutes later, I heard his call sign over the radio: "Showtime one-two, Miller time, Miller time," the standard call indicating he'd dropped his bombs and was heading out of the target area. (As in, "Mission complete—it's Miller time!"; time for a beer.)

Using our radars to regroup into formation, we turned back toward safety, polishing off another group of red air on the way out. Mission complete and running low on fuel, we turned toward home. The rest of the flight was uneventful. We landed, finished our paperwork, and headed to the debrief.

It went well. My first months at TOPGUN had taught me to be thorough in a debrief, so I took care to describe the lessons learned during the administrative and mission portions of the flight. With a member of the red air joining us in the room, we discussed the dogfights that had occurred both inbound to and outbound from the target—all red air destroyed and both blue fighters remaining alive—always the best outcome.

At this point, we moved into discussing performance within the target area. My instructor had successfully destroyed the two aircraft with simulated GPS-guided bombs, taking them both out in my absence. All in all, a good result equating to mission accomplished.

I had completed my portion of the debrief. My instructor now took over to cover whatever I'd missed. There was always something, no matter how hard I tried.

He walked through some things I'd missed and clarified some techniques to make us better on our next flight before getting to the punch line: I'd have to fly the mission again. Though we had satisfied the overall mission objectives, I hadn't reached the target area, and he needed to assess my ability to properly release weapons before I could advance to the next flight. All in all, however, the flight had gone well for one reason: an abundantly clear briefing.

"Bus, nice work today with the brief," he told me. "It's altogether too common for students to get bogged down with all the details required for a self-escort strike flight. More often than not, students will spend too much time in one section and run out of time to brief the remainder. You avoided that problem today."

"More importantly," he said, "you put the most important part of the brief at the very front and made it crystal clear: target destruction was required, a fact you emphasized several more times. This meant that, when we became separated, I knew my responsibility was to get to the target before our window of opportunity closed. If you'd failed to mention that, it'd be a mission failure instead of a success."

His words stayed with me—**_don't bury the lead._**

It wasn't until my first job at the Pentagon that I learned the military term for this: put the bottom line up front (written as "BLUF"). Most senior officers and their staffs were prone to sending long status updates via email, a necessity when covering a multitude of complicated topics, *but* almost without fail, at the top of these senior leaders' emails was BLUF, followed by a succinct recap of the most important elements of their message. The rest of the update followed. It was a way to ensure that senior leaders didn't miss the most important takeaway, which was more likely if the nuggets were scattered throughout.

My own boss, the chief of naval operations, continually reminded me to stop burying the lead with speeches I wrote for him. My natural flow in a speech was to lay out the background first—then get to the "so what."

I soon learned to put the most important material up front and then provide any amplifying information later in his speech. In fact, I would cover the most important material three times: once at the beginning, once in the middle as I provided explanation, and again in the conclusion as a reminder. His guidance, coupled with what I had learned at TOPGUN, held me in good stead for the rest of my career.

Put the Bottom Line Up Front

In our information-saturated society, with so much material vying for our attention, it's easy for important pieces of information to get lost in the noise. Effective communication is one of the most difficult daily tasks for any leader, whether in or out of uniform. Getting an entire organization aligned and working together toward mission success is difficult enough. Do all you can to make your team's lives easier. Put your BLUF at the beginning of your messages, emails, and discussions.

Learn to communicate the most important messages early—and often—to help those around you understand what you care about most.

Don't bury the lead—always ***put the bottom line up front***.

Officers from Strike Fighter Squadron ONE NINE FIVE with their counterparts from a Japanese Air Self-Defense Forces F-4 Phantom II squadron at Hyakuri Air Base in Japan in 2015 (author is front and center).

CHAPTER TEN

DON'T WAIT TO MAKE A FRIEND UNTIL YOU NEED ONE

> " Build personal connections early and often. Not because you need anything but because you genuinely want to learn more about them. "

I STRODE INTO THE conference room. Today was a big day: time to make a quantum leap in air warfare tactics. I was also about to learn that one of my most important lessons had little to do with maneuvering a high-performance fighter jet—and everything to do with working well as part of a team.

As the unit's air-to-air mission planning subject matter expert, I was responsible for the timelines used by the U.S. Navy and Marines Corps—a significant undertaking because of the sheer amount of information involved. Aviators use timelines to determine how, and at what ranges, they will take actions while fighting, all based on their adversaries' aircraft capabilities, altitude, and airspeed. Timelines provide aviators with the rules for when to complete specific actions in air-to-air combat, from how far away to target and shoot an adversary, and when to maneuver their aircraft into a preemptive defense to avoid being shot.

For the past seven months, I'd hustled to transition the TOPGUN staff from its dependence on 1980s, Soviet-era, air-to-air tactics to a far more advanced, updated version necessary to defeat the newest fighters and missiles from other adversary nations' air forces. My predecessor on staff had proposed using lessons culled from the U.S. Air Force's recent experiences but had departed before any formal changes were made. Now, the burden was on me to conduct the research and create the new timelines required for the Navy and Marine Corps to jump forward.

The first six months were part of my murderboard process. I'd worked with other intelligence agencies—the CIA, the National Air and Space Intelligence Center, and the Defense Intelligence Agency—to study and refine new tactics and timelines. I'd simplified the 1980s-era timelines—collapsing three separate timelines into one—and created several new variations to reestablish our competitive edge. A vast majority of that work was formally adopted when I passed my murderboard. But a decision about the most significant change—a new timeline for extremely advanced threats—had been postponed to give the Standardization Board time for further study.

We were devoting today's standardization meeting largely to revisiting and voting on the advanced timeline.

The training officer kicked off the meeting before turning the floor over to me. Since this was a complicated subject involving pages of numbers, I used a slideshow, leading the assembled team through the ins and outs of why our tactics needed revision—and why this new timeline was the way to do it. Luckily, this wasn't a murderboard, so I was free to look at the slides as needed.

Only five minutes into my briefing, the first hand shot up into the air.

"I don't get it," said one instructor. "Why did that number change so significantly from last year?"

I walked him through the math, explaining how a new adversary missile had changed the game, putting our fighters at increased risk.

Another hand went up.

"Hang on," said the standardization officer. "Shouldn't these two numbers and that third one on the previous slide be connected?"

No, I answered, because they represented two separate classes of aircraft with drastically different capabilities. He leaned back in his chair, a thoughtful frown affixed to his face.

I quickly realized this wasn't going well. Instructors asked question after question—and they were increasingly detailed. We were going down rabbit holes and losing sight of the big picture. I doubted whether, at this rate, I'd get the votes needed to pass the newest—and much needed—timeline.

Three thoughts hit me as I stood at the podium, listening to the raging debate:

1. Isn't this material obvious? The math is straightforward.

2. Even if the math doesn't make sense, just trust me—this is my area of expertise.

3. My first two thoughts are ridiculous.

I'd lost sight of the fact that I had immersed myself in this problem for seven months. What was obvious to me wasn't obvious to others who were seeing this information for the first time. On top of this, my audience was responsible for issuing tactical changes with far-reaching ramifications. They had a professional requirement to challenge my assumptions and underlying math until they were satisfied—and shouldn't stop until I had convinced a majority of the Standardization Board that this was the correct way to operate.

One thing was certain: I had failed to lay the groundwork required for my own—and the staff's—success. We had all arrived to make a substantive decision, but the information I was presenting was so technical that one meeting wasn't going to provide enough time to answer everyone's questions, let alone vote to publish the new timeline.

I had made an unforced error.

Two hours later, we left the conference room disgruntled. With staff members running at capacity, meetings like these needed to flow more smoothly. We didn't have the time to waste.

Our next meeting on the new timeline was to be held the following month, so I set to work.

I made one critical change to my process based on my earlier observations: during the next three weeks, I sat down one-on-one with the ten Standardization Board members to talk about the new timeline, offered insight from my research, and—most importantly—listened to their questions and concerns. I quickly realized that every instructor was interested in a different angle. Their questions ranged from the simplest to the most complex.

I also researched fully each one of their concerns. When we finished the day's flight schedule, I'd sit with each individual to answer their questions, happy to take on any follow-up questions.

In less than a month, I'd contacted and answered the questions of every Standardization Board member.

During the second group meeting, things flowed far

more smoothly. My briefing to the instructors felt more like I was just going through the motions—heads were nodding in agreement, and there were far fewer questions. Most inquiries were about broad generalities or to discuss additional changes to our tactics likely to be affected by the new timeline. This time, there were no challenging questions, as they'd all been handled privately before we arrived. Each member's concerns had been asked, answered, and in some cases shared with others to generate consensus before we ever walked into the room.

I quickly realized that, while success is never guaranteed, a person can take proactive steps to narrow the odds as much as possible. Fostering alignment within the team is one of those steps. Recognizing that persuading your peers—other leaders—to follow your lead requires finesse, not a pronouncement.

This lesson made a significant impact on my personal and professional lives. I began engaging early with others to get to know them, understand their concerns and goals, and build rapport with them long before we needed to discuss business. I worked to anticipate their concerns, creating solutions that incorporated their views from the very beginning. This paid dividends.

For example, as one of eight squadron commanders in our Japan-based air wing, I conferred early and often with my peers before making a formal recommendation. That proved critical. I created a new way to conduct training that saved the U.S. Navy $15 million per year, reduced wear and tear on our jets, and enabled aircrew to train more effectively. Working with other commanding officers behind the scenes meant I was able to hand my boss—the air wing commander—a fully reviewed plan that I could say had the backing of a majority of my peers. This proactive approach made it easy for him to approve the changes.

Beyond that, our air wing shared an air base with members of the Japanese Air Self-Defense Force (Japan's air force). Usually, the Americans and Japanese kept to themselves. I broke this mold by reaching across the flight line and to other bases in the region, which led to the creation of a new cooperative training program, one that included American and Japanese fighter pilots. For the first time in decades, we began training, socializing, and flying missions together. We forged stronger ties—ties that will prove critical if our nations fight alongside each other in the future.

Making friends early and coordinating often with them also worked best when I was *not* the senior leader in the room. That was the case when I worked at the Pentagon as Secretary Mattis's communications director. Mattis could tell people what he wanted them to do. As a Navy commander, I didn't have that authority. Instead, I worked behind the scenes to align interests, so big initiatives, like writing and publishing the groundbreaking 2018 National Defense Strategy, became much easier to accomplish.

In fact, knowing that such a significant change in our national strategy would raise concerns on Capitol Hill, we shared an early draft version with a person from each side of the aisle—a Democrat and a Republican. The rewards were twofold: first, these individuals provided valuable feedback. Second, even if we didn't incorporate their input, we built goodwill simply by asking for their opinions.

When we unveiled the strategy, we received rare bipartisan praise.

Too often in life, we reach out and introduce ourselves to others only when we need something. When we work that way, we find that our chance of success is greatly diminished, especially when working with our peers. Who hasn't been turned off by the person who pays little attention to you until there's something they need and then you suddenly become their favorite person?

So, get out of your comfort zone. Build personal connections early and often. Not because you need anything but because you genuinely want to learn more about them. You'll realize that getting to know others and working behind the scenes to ensure their concerns are met can lead to some amazing results, regardless of whether you're at work, in the community, or with your family.

As an old African proverb states, "If you want to go fast, go alone…if you want to go far, go together." You'll find that you can accomplish so much more when you take the time to invest in others around you, especially when you seek nothing in return. Over time, this approach helps to build the consensus and support needed to achieve team wins, and not just personal wins.

To achieve your best results, ***don't wait to make a friend until you need one***.

The author giving his change of command speech at Naval Air Facility Atsugi, Japan, in December 2016.

EPILOGUE

THE LESSONS I learned at TOPGUN made all the difference during my career, both in and out of uniform.

In the fall of 2018, I retired as a U.S. Navy commander. It was a challenging time for me and for my family, as the path we had expected to stay on suddenly changed, throwing everything into chaos. I'd been offered a senior-level job in the Pentagon, only to have it pulled away at the last moment (and after I'd made other life-altering decisions to accept it). In the span of a month, I needed to find a new job, move the family to a new house, and figure out a new path for my life—and that was all before I suffered a herniated disc in my neck resulting from years of flying a fighter jet.

Stressful stuff, even in the best of times. But I quickly fell back on the lessons I share in this book: staying calm, anticipating problems, relying on my wingmen, and receiving support from friends I'd made along the way during a twenty-year career. I appreciated that people I'd never met offered their support based solely on my reputation or because they trusted the person recommending me to them.

By using these tools, I was able to move quickly. In the first year after retiring, I started my own company, wrote my first book, became a national security commentator on television, joined the boards of directors for several nonprofit companies I am passionate about, started a podcast (*Holding the Line*), and began speaking publicly about many of the lessons you have just read. In fact, the positive reception I received after sharing these lessons is what led to this, my second book.

The value of many of these lessons had been reinforced to me in 2011, when I was stationed with my family in Japan during my first tour of duty following TOPGUN.

On March 11 of that year, a 9.1-magnitude earthquake struck Sendai, Japan, located about 250 miles northeast of Naval Air Facility Atsugi, our base near Tokyo. Despite our distance from the epicenter, we still registered a 6.7. I'll never forget standing on the second floor of a hangar, talking to my commanding officer, when I saw the trees and telephone poles begin to sway like reeds in the wind. Shortly thereafter, a powerful tsunami struck the east coast of Japan. I watched the television in my office with sorrow as walls of water destroyed homes and critically damaged the Fukushima Daiichi Nuclear Power Plant. Three of the six nuclear units exploded during the next several days as several reactor cores melted down, spewing clouds of radioactive material into the air.

People panicked. Nuclear fallout is invisible. You can't see it, but its effects are real, so people went into survival mode. Supplies of toilet paper, gasoline, and food were quickly exhausted. Cities across Japan experienced rolling blackouts due to multiple power plants being taken offline. Families were instructed to stay indoors, shut all windows, and turn off their air-conditioning when the winds shifted toward us from the power plant. Commercial jets commissioned by the U.S. State Department lined our base's runway to fly families to safety, while service members conducted a no-notice evacuation of aircraft to other bases in the region. Uncertainty reigned and families were unsure of what to do.

Sound familiar? The coronavirus pandemic of 2019–2020 reminds me of the Fukushima disaster, except the pandemic is affecting every nation around the globe with longer-lasting impacts. This experience reinforces my belief that these lessons—learned over the course of decades—apply to any number of situations, from the most personal to those that are wide-ranging in nature.

The response to the pandemic demonstrates the critical necessity for leaders around the world to be guided by a professional and ethical North Star, to put service before self, to embrace honesty, and to stay calm under pressure. The chaos created by an out-of-nowhere virus could have been lessened had senior leaders anticipated problems and taken proactive steps to counter the spread, instead of reacting belatedly and only after the problem grew out of control.

Though few of us will have an outsize impact on the world as a whole, that doesn't mean we can't use the lessons described in this book to help guide our own behavior during times of crisis, be they global or personal. As financial expert Dave Ramsey is prone to saying, "What happens in *your* house is far more important than what happens in the White House." Success in life is an individual responsibility.

The pandemic forced many countries to put in place some form of quarantine and social distancing, pushing hundreds of millions of people around the world to begin working from home. This led to additional challenges, as day care and schools were also forced to shut down, placing added pressure on working parents. The job market remains uncertain with more than fourteen million people unemployed at the height of the outbreak. Millions of students saw their high school and college graduations canceled.

Much like my experience with transitioning out of

uniform, the lessons in this book can help you *thrive* in a chaotic environment, not merely survive. In many ways, adjusting to the realities of the pandemic is reminiscent of life onboard an aircraft carrier.

Modern deployments last, on average, from seven to nine months at a time. Forty-five hundred sailors become your new extended family while sailing in a warship across open oceans. It's exciting at first, waving goodbye to anxious family members as the carrier pulls away from the pier and steams into the distance. The first week or two flies by as the crew focuses on their assigned tasks, the newness and adrenaline taking the edge off the fact you're crammed into close quarters like tuna in a can.

But after a month, life turns monotonous as you perform the same tasks day after day, week after week. I considered myself one of the lucky ones, as I was afforded the chance to launch skyward each day to fly a new mission, leaving behind the metallic smells and loud noises for an hour or two.

Everyone is on edge by the time the third month rolls around. Miraculously, this moment of maximum frustration is also when the crew begins to adjust for the long haul, a situation we routinely referred to as "finding our happy place." Sailors begin to renew their focus, new friendships are forged, and everyone realizes that the only way to survive is to pull together as one tight-knit community. The daily routine is embraced and becomes second nature. Another benefit is the ability to reflect, plan, and become more creative, as there are only so many movies you can watch or card games you can play in an attempt to ward off boredom.

So, too, with our experience during the pandemic.

Families have been forced to embark on their own "deployments," working from home in confined spaces. The novelty quickly wore off, stress levels climbed, and everyone soon reached peak frustration.

But families, like the sailors I served with, can adapt. Anticipating problems is now a way of life when navigating an uncertain future. Living in close quarters—all day, every day—is forging stronger bonds for teamwork and support. Parents are becoming more in tune with their children. In some cases, families are growing closer as grandparents—the wingmen—volunteer to spend more time quarantined with their grandchildren, freeing parents to refocus on their jobs. The upside is that with so much work being conducted online, over the phone, or via conference calls, it's now easier than ever to plan out tomorrow's schedule, along with the rest of the week. Consistency lends itself to finding a rhythm where productivity climbs and frustrations begin to fall away.

Gaining efficiencies while working remotely can provide you with a lot of opportunity, but it requires focus. Make the most of this opportunity. Learn a new skill. Invest in long conversations with your friends and family. And my favorite: instead of surfing the web or watching TV in your down time, pull out a pad of paper and jot down notes about your future. Where do you want to be in one year? five years? ten years?

Thinking this far into the future becomes a part of your personal strategy. Once you've defined your specific goals, it becomes much easier to think backward for intermediate steps you will need to accomplish to get there. Let's say you want to earn a master's degree within five years. With this as your long-term goal, you now know that you need to answer a few questions: What do you want to study? Where would you like to attend college? How much will it cost? What else is required to make this particular dream a reality?

Then, you simply back up: What are the biggest obstacles to success? In this case, money is one of the most obvious issues. So, how much will it cost? What does your savings plan, scholarship potential, company support, or student loan situation look like? Knowing how much you'll need and where the money will come from helps you put a plan in place to make it all work.

This is one specific example. In every case—and across every possible scenario—thinking long-term enables you to take actions now to help bring you one step closer to your future goal. Life normally keeps us too busy to think deeply about our future, so use the opportunities created by the pandemic to slow down and reinvest in yourself.

I'm also reminded that just like our half-year deployments, times of adversity never last forever. Despite all the hardship and stress, eventually the aircraft carrier pulls back into port when the cruise ends, with everyone onboard stronger for the experience. When times of adversity draw to an end, have you not only survived…but found a way to *thrive*?

Whatever your particular situation, always remember: nothing worthwhile is ever easy. Our success—and the success of our communities, companies, and far beyond—depends on the willingness of each and every one of us to do our very best, even during the times when no one is looking. *Especially* when no one is looking. You may never know how doing your very best positively affects those around you, but I guarantee that it does. Remember: your actions always speak louder than your words ever can.

So, buckle up, work hard, inspire others through your example…and ***never wait to make a difference***.

READING LIST

A DEDICATION TO LIFELONG learning positively impacts your ability to create success in life. For most, this includes a voracious appetite for reading. Reading on a regular basis broadens our horizons, increases our level of knowledge, and enables us to learn from the experience and knowledge of others. In short, it's one of the best—and most proven—ways to greatly accelerate your chosen career path. Most importantly, by reading widely you're given the chance to learn from the mistakes of others without having to suffer from your own avoidable setbacks—which can be an absolute game changer.

Reading has made all the difference in my life. In

many ways, I've become a melting pot reflecting the knowledge gained from the books I've read and the leaders I've interacted with. I'm sure the same is true for you.

Here are some of the books that made a significant difference in my life as I grew and developed as a leader in my own right. I share these with you as yet another way to continue along your own path of lifelong learning.

Likewise, I'd love to learn more about the books that have made a difference to you. Please feel free to send me a note on Twitter using my handle, @guysnodgrass, with your favorite reads.

The Emperor's Handbook, Marcus Aurelius
How to Win Friends and Influence People, Dale Carnegie
The 7 Habits of Highly Effective People, Steven R. Covey
How to Become CEO: The Rules for Rising to the Top of Any Organization, Jeffrey J. Fox
David and Goliath, Malcolm Gladwell
Made to Stick: Why Some Ideas Survive and Others Die, Chip Heath and Dan Heath

Reading List

Think and Grow Rich, Napoleon Hill

Make Your Bed, Admiral William H. McRaven, (U.S. Navy Retired)

Goals! How to Get Everything You Want—Faster Than You Ever Thought Possible, Brian Tracy

The Purpose Driven Life: What on Earth Am I Here For?, Rick Warren

Magazines and newspapers are another inexhaustible source of knowledge and awareness about the world around us. While I'll leave it to you to pursue the news sources of your choice, I do offer one word of advice: be willing to read across the ideological spectrum and challenge your own worldview.

Today's highly polarized environment is causing tremendous internal strife in America, a situation made worse by people only reading from sources that simply amplify their current beliefs. Instead, seek to broaden your horizons by reading from diverse sources: *New York Times* as well as the *Wall Street Journal*, or watching both CNN and Fox News (as an example). Also seek out international sources like the BBC or *The Economist*, which will enable you to better understand how America looks through the eyes of others.

In so doing, you'll gain a more holistic awareness of the world around you while developing a greater tolerance for one unchangeable fact: not everyone sees the world in exactly the same way. Being able to articulate your own beliefs while understanding and accepting those of others is a powerful tool for success!

ACKNOWLEDGMENTS

EVERYTHING OF SIGNIFICANCE that I accomplished during my career was made possible only through the tireless support I've received from family and friends. I am again reminded that a strong support network is a proven force multiplier, enabling accomplishments far beyond what I could ever hope to achieve on my own.

I was lucky to have several people willing to provide additional research, insight, and feedback along the way. Retired U.S. Navy Cmdr. Vincent "Jell-O" Aiello, a fellow TOPGUN instructor and host of the always-inspiring *Fighter Pilot Podcast*, kept me on the straight and narrow by meticulously fact-checking each chapter.

Acknowledgments

His efforts ensured that I told my stories with accuracy and precision. Thank you to many others who offered their mentorship and perspective: Fred Rainbow, Lee Snodgrass, Veronica Overman, and Steve Cohen.

I was fortunate that Steve Cohen introduced me to Lisa Leshne and Sam Morrice of the Leshne Agency. Lisa and Sam provided tireless support during the production of this book, as did Center Street's Daisy Hutton, Kate Hartson, and Sean McGowan.

To my wife, Sarah, and my mother, Sherri, for providing honest feedback at every step along the way: thank you for your willingness to read every word of this book—multiple times.

This book is dedicated to my father, Marvin Snodgrass, who passed away in 2013. Even from my earliest memories he was adamant about learning to live a life of purpose. Those lessons—the importance of putting others before myself, maintaining an ethical compass that points true north, and always "leaving the campsite better than I found it"—served as the foundation upon which all other lessons were built. I'll always appreciate his constant reminder that our most precious resource

Acknowledgments

is time: it's the one thing we can never get more of…and once we've spent it, we can never get it back.

Lastly, to the many men and women I was honored to serve alongside during my time in uniform: thank you for serving as steady reminders of the values that make America's experiment in democracy both vibrant and resilient.

America will always need patriots willing to put service before self.

CPSIA information can be obtained
at www.ICGtesting.com
Printed in the USA
LVHW081759230123
737762LV00018B/706/J

9 781546 059639